REAL PRISON
REAL FREEDOM

REAL PRISON
REAL FREEDOM

Rosser McDonald

ELM HILL

A Division of
HarperCollins Christian Publishing

www.elmhillbooks.com

Real Prison
Real Freedom

Published in Nashville, Tennessee, by Elm Hill, an imprint of Thomas Nelson. Elm Hill and Thomas Nelson are registered trademarks of HarperCollins Christian Publishing, Inc.

Elm Hill titles may be purchased in bulk for educational, business, fund-raising, or sales promotional use. For information, please e-mail SpecialMarkets@ ThomasNelson.com.

Library of Congress Cataloging-in-Publication Data

Library of Congress Control Number: 2019921045

ISBN 978-1-400330652 (Advance Reading Copy)

ISBN 978-1-400330348 (Paperback)
ISBN 978-1-400330355 (Hardbound)
ISBN 978-1-400330362 (eBook)

CHAPTER ONE

"What is the nature of the motion?"

"Your Honor, the state has a motion to try him in restraints, now and throughout this trial."

"Let's hear whatever evidence you want to present. The court has a standing order not to try inmates in restraints. Unless you have evidence to convince me he should be, he will not be."

"We have evidence and we're ready to put them on now, if the court so desires."

"Let's do it, now," Judge Melvin Whitaker said and shifted in the high-backed leather chair, as if some quick movements might speed things up. The judge was anxious to get preliminaries out of the way. The jurors were milling about the halls and Judge Whitaker was always antsy about keeping them waiting.

Prosecutor Mark Patterson of the Special Prison Prosecution Unit called for Warden Richard Waldron.

As the warden stood up, so did the anxious young defense attorney, Neil Durrance. "Your Honor, we would object. I think this motion is untimely."

"The objection is overruled."

Warden Waldron glanced to his left as he walked through the door in the mahogany railing that separated the audience from the official proceedings. He saw the defendant, Rickie Smith, and his lawyer, then

1

walked to the right, passing the prosecutor and his investigator. They all shared the same large, sturdy table in this courtroom, instead of the usual separate tables for prosecution and defense.

Patterson led Waldron through the basics, over continuing objections by the defense attorney.

Waldron was warden of the Eastham Unit of the Texas Department of Corrections, commonly called TDC. He began as a guard fourteen years ago and became a warden three years ago, assigned to Eastham.

He explained that's when he met Rickie Smith.

Patterson asked, "Warden Waldron: Does inmate Smith, to your knowledge, have a reputation inside of TDC?"

"His reputation is one of being unpredictable, extremely violent, murderous, uncontrollable."

"In your personal experience with inmate Smith, has that reputation been backed up?"

"Yes!"

The prosecutor and the witness then went through a list of persons in the courtroom to establish that the judge, jurors, attorneys, investigator, and the court reporter were all only a few feet from the defendant and vulnerable if he should be able to attack.

"And in your experience, would he be the type that might use something sitting right here on a table or here in the courtroom as a weapon?"

"If he had access to it—yes, sir."

"In your opinion, would it be safe to have inmate Smith sitting here without restraints while witnesses testify from that box and while the jury was over here in this trial?"

"Again, sir, considering the unpredictability of his behavior—no sir, I do not believe it would be safe for those people."

In cross examination, defense attorney Durrance tried to soften the harshness of the warden's assertion by asking him if he knew of any time that Rickie Smith had attacked a judge or jurors or anyone else in a courtroom. The warden admitted he did not know of Smith being violent outside of prison. Durrance had the warden describe how six armed prison guards as well as the court bailiff were positioned near the defendant and around the courtroom. Then, they described the routine of searching inmate Smith and going through a metal detector before entering the courtroom.

Next, the prosecution called John Bonner, assistant regional director of TDC in charge of transportation and security of inmates for medical and court appointments. Over defense objections, Patterson asked, "In terms of other inmates reputations that you know of in TDC regarding violence and assaultiveness, where would this man's range?"

Bonner stated firmly, "He would be one of the most assaultive that we have in TDC!"

"How many people are you aware of that he has stabbed since he's been in TDC?"

Durrance stood to his feet, "Your Honor, I would object. I think this brings in extraneous offenses."

Judge Whitaker looked at the attorney, "It would be a good objection before the jury but before the court, it's overruled."

Bonner stated, "Personally, I am aware of about five officers that he has assaulted."

Patterson then had Bonner describe how inmate Smith had brought a knife into a disciplinary hearing and—even though he had been searched—stabbed two officers. The setting was compared to the current courtroom scene.

"Would the safety of the judge, the witnesses, the court reporter, the jurors, and the other people inside the bar—would the safety of these people be in serious jeopardy if inmate Smith was left without restraints?"

"Anyone inside this courtroom would be in danger with Rickie Smith."

The prosecution put on other witnesses, adding weight to Rickie Smith's reputation as extremely, unpredictably, but expectedly violent. Defense Attorney Durrance tried over and over, unsuccessfully, to keep the testimony out of court. In desperation he tried another strategy which had an even worse effect. He asked questions designed to show that

Smith's attacks were only directed at guards in retaliation to mistreatment he had suffered.

Durrance obviously was not fully aware of his client's record. Several questions he hoped would show a lack of violence actually became ambushes. The answers told of even more attacks and threats made by the defendant. Trying to soften Bonner's testimony about Rickie Smith stabbing two officers in a disciplinary hearing, Durrance asked about transportation, Bonner's current responsibility, "Are you aware of any incident involving a breach of security involving the transport of Mr. Smith to and from the courtroom?"

Bonner shocked the court, "There was a possible incident in transporting inmate Smith sometime—I believe it was in 1984—where the Texas Rangers received information that there would be a breakout of inmate Smith on the Trinity River Bridge. They were going to block both ends of the bridge, kill our officers, and break him out of the van."

The lawyer tried to recover, "Did they cross the Trinity River Bridge that day?"

"After the Texas Rangers arrested the other inmates involved, who were out on parole, and brought them back to the department, we made it through that incident without any problem."

"And, in fact, Mr. Smith did not escape; is that correct?"

"Due to our information received prior to, yes!"

Trying to separate 1984 and today, four years later, Durrance asked, "Have you received any information about this trial, here, today?"

"Yes, I have."

Obviously not the answer the attorney hoped for. "Have you taken measures to prevent that?"

"That's why you see the number of officers that you do."

Durrance seemed a little dazed and wandered through some rather inane questions about security procedures before giving up. He passed the witness back to the prosecutor, who dug the hole deeper by leading Bonner to say that Rickie Smith was a known member of the Aryan Brotherhood Prison Gang.

Next, Chief Deputy Sheriff Jimbo Rains was called. He told of taking Rickie Smith to a courthouse for a hearing and when returning him to the Diagnostic Unit of Texas Prisons, Smith, although stripped to his boxer shorts and socks, produced an improvised knife and stabbed another inmate.

Again, the defense attorney tried to soften the impact by isolating the incident in prison and only involving another inmate. Instead, it got worse. Smith had to push the sheriff out of the way to get to Ernest Ross who was in handcuffs, leg irons, and belly chain.

Finally, Wes Savage came to the stand. Savage worked in TDC in the Special Transportation Unit. He testified that two weeks before, he brought Rickie Smith to the court for a hearing in this case and in a room adjacent to the courtroom, he heard Smith say that if he lost this case, "the rest of them were for free." Savage explained that meant if he loses this case, "officers or guards on any farm that inmate Smith is on has no protection from him."

Between the prosecution and the defense, Judge Whitaker was left with little choice. He had to break his own longstanding policy of letting inmates sit in court like any other citizen.

"Based on the evidence that I've heard, the court finds that it is necessary to try the defendant in restraints. I think you will probably need to make some arrangements. I will give you an option about it. He can sit at the end of the table, cover his hands, and keep his feet away from the jury and not be displayed before the jury, unless he does it himself."

Durrance asked if Smith could at least have his hands free to write notes and communicate. Judge Whitaker said he was convinced Smith's hands should not be free, adding, "I might say that I tried this inmate in Anderson County where he was charged with stabbing a correctional officer. The jury found him guilty. I've also had communication from your client indicating that he was trying his best to get to death row. That he was going to keep on sticking people, and he did. The primary concern of the court is the security of anyone who happens to be present. If you need time to stop and talk with him along the way, we'll break and do that. I'm going to require him to stay in restraints during the trial."

"Why don't you just move me out of here and let me go back to my cell if you're going to try me in restraints? It's the same thing," the defendant yelled. The judge barely glanced at Smith. He was perturbed that the delay was dragging on and on while the jurors waited in the halls, wondering what was going on.

Durrance moved for a delay in the trial so he could find rebuttal witnesses. He called the motion to use restraints an ambush. He argued with the prosecutor and the judge, who overruled the motion for delay. The attorney again moved for a mistrial.

"I think counsel is aware that this is an exception. I can't recall ever trying an inmate in this courtroom in restraints, but I've never had the evidence that I have before me in this case. The court notes your exceptions and they are respectfully overruled."

After more arguing, Judge Whitaker called for a 15-minute recess and then the beginning of the trial. This is one of eight such charges filed in Houston County alone against Rickie Smith.

The much-discussed "restraints" consisted of leg shackles with a chain less than 2 feet long, handcuffs attached to a belly chain which kept arms from being extended, and a "black box" which was fastened over the hands to keep them apart and unable to grasp anything. All that paraphernalia was put in place before dawn as part of the normal ritual when an inmate was going to leave his "Super Segregation" cell.

What the judge probably still does not know is that he made a very wise decision. The fact is that Rickie Smith had a homemade knife hidden on his body that day—in spite of all the security precautions. His plan was to attack someone with it. His first-choice target was Royce Smithey—an investigator with the Texas governor's Special Prosecutor's Office—who was seated with the prosecution team at the other end of the table from the defendant.

"Super Segregation" is the name given a row of a dozen cells specially modified to create the most segregated, highest security block of the Texas prison system. They house the most difficult and dangerous twelve inmates in Texas prisons at the time. Another unit has six such "SuperSeg" cells.

How does one qualify for such distinction? How does Rickie Smith rate as the most feared of the eighteen?

The answers are to be found in the Rickie Smith story.

It is not a simple story. It involves love and hate, despair and hope, criminality and honesty, immorality and honor. All those words and more apply to Rickie Smith. In addition, his story intersects the life stories of others—including lovers, criminals, an unorthodox warden, God, and Satan.

An integral part of the story is twenty-five years of turmoil in Texas Prisons. It began with a federal judge's declaration that the Texas Department of Corrections prisons were "inhumane mistreatment centers" and he oversaw the reluctant transition to kinder, gentler human warehouses. Concurrently, the inmate population grew 700 percent.

While telling the 'what' of the story, we also search for the 'how' and 'why.'

CHAPTER TWO

I n the wee hours Christmas morning, 1954, Betty called out, "It's time and I'm ready to go!" Selestia Smith jumped out of bed while Red struggled to cut through the fog in his brain, leftover from the Christmas Eve party that ended just a couple of hours ago.

Selestia yelled, "We'll be right there. Come on Red, we've got to go to the hospital!"

Red complied with his body, but his mind was trying to grasp what this meant. The Smiths had been married ten years, but Selestia could not get pregnant after having a miscarriage with complications. Red had agreed to adopt and had accepted that Betty's baby would become theirs. Now, it was sobering—literally—to face a reality which his mind had kept in the abstract. Betty was seventeen and agreed to give her baby to the Smiths. She moved in with them to await the birth. Within 10 minutes, the Smiths took Betty and her overnight bag and headed for North Shore Hospital in Pasadena.

T. R. Smith, Red to most everyone, was a competent construction superintendent in Houston, Texas. His abilities were getting recognized and he was getting hired on progressively bigger building projects. Houston was booming, thanks to the petroleum industry and the post-World War 2 economic growth. Red met Selestia Lay at a party and they married soon after. He nicknamed her "Torchie" but she never liked it. After a while, Selestia became less interested in the parties and drinking that Red earned a reputation for. She wanted to be a mother and home maker and wished that Red would become more domesticated, too. It was beginning to cause tension in the marriage. Selestia just knew that a baby would fix everything.

"It's a boy, Mr. and Mrs. Smith," the doctor announced.

They followed him to the nursery window for their first look at Rickie. Betty had insisted that the paperwork be done so that as soon as the baby was born, it would become theirs. "He's just the sweetest little thing you ever saw," Selestia said. "The best Christmas present I ever got."

Being parents took Torchie pretty much off the party circuit, but it didn't slow Red down very much. People marveled at how he could party so much but always be on the job bright and early, apparently without a hangover. He never lacked for party friends—male and female—even though they moved frequently to different parts of Houston and its sub-urbs as he finished projects. Many of them were people who worked for him or with him.

Rickie's early childhood was normal. They always lived in a com-fortable house with neighborhood friends to play with. He got plenty of love from a doting mother, which seemed to make up for any lack of interest from his dad. Actually, Red grew to love Rickie but he just didn't know what to do with a child. He was geared to being strong, able to take care of himself and knowing what to do—like a good superintendent. Children don't automatically fit into a real man's world.

Whether by nature or from his dad's encouragement, or both, Rickie was what you'd call 'all boy' climbing onto things, exploring, trying to see how things work. His earliest childhood memory was climbing on the barbecue in the backyard and falling off at about three years old. There was blood all over from a busted mouth. Mom consoled him and applied first aid, but he got little sympathy when Dad got home.

Not long after he started school, Rickie was with Timmy, a neighbor who was a year or two older.

"You're an illegitimate," Timmy said.

"Why do you say that?" Rickie demanded.

"Because them ain't your real parents and that makes you illegitimate." Timmy's mother had noticed that Rickie's hair was brown but both parents had red hair and she asked about it. Selestia told her Rickie was adopted and apparently Timmy got the news, too.

Rickie had noticed the hair difference himself, but he wasn't about to stand for such a name-calling. He picked up a stick and cracked Timmy over the head a few times. When the stick broke, he used his fists. He was pounding the boy good when Timmy's mother came out and pulled Rickie off. He ran home crying and asked his mom if it was true, "Am I a bastard?" he demanded.

"Who told you that?"

"Timmy," Rickie replied.

His red-haired mother took up the fight, running out of the house with Rickie on her heels. When the lady came to the door, Selestia pulled her out of the house by her hair and gave her a whipping like Timmy got. Then she picked up Rickie and carried him home.

They sat down and she explained that she did not give birth to him, but she loved him and was his mother just the same. Rickie said he knew she was his mother from that day on. However, as most adopted kids do, he sometimes wondered what was wrong with him that his real mother gave him away.

Another time, Rickie was scuffling with another boy who busted him in the nose. Rickie ran home to his dad with the blood running out.

"Don't you cry and run home, boy. Defend yourself."

Rickie sniffled, "He's older than me, Dad."

"Next time, don't come running home or I'll whup you. I want you to stand up and be a man," he said. "Get a stick and make him eat it if you have to."

A few days later, it happened again. So Rickie obeyed. He found a stick and literally tried to make the other boy eat it. Rickie had it sticking in the boy's mouth when the mother, a large woman, came out and pulled Rickie off. When he went home and told what had happened, Red charged over to the boy's house and had an argument with his dad. They ended up fighting in the yard. At least Red showed he was proud of his son and took up for him that time.

School was a real challenge for Rickie Smith. He did fine in the first grade and OK in the second. By the third grade he was falling behind. Spelling and reading were just about impossible for him. A school teacher, Mrs. Green, called his parents to the school and tried to convince them something was wrong with Rickie.

"There's nothing wrong with him," Red declared angrily.

He decided that he would take care of the situation. He would give Rickie a list of words and lock him in a room to learn to spell them. When Rickie still couldn't spell them, Red would take his belt in the room and use it, trying to force Rickie to learn.

Tippy, a pit bulldog, wasn't about to let anyone whip Rickie. When Red started with the belt, Tippy attacked and bit Red, who went to get his gun to kill him. But Selestia said he would have to shoot her, too, and she got between him and the dog. So Red would lock Tippy in the garage before the tutoring sessions. When Tippy heard Rickie yelling, he'd try to break through the garage door. He bloodied his nose and head trying to get out to protect his master.

Selestia decided she had to take Tippy's place. One evening when Red took Rickie into the room with his belt and some spelling words, she got an ax and went out to the window of the room and hollered, "If you touch him with that belt, I'll cut this window in and we're going to have trouble!"

Red relented and that was the end of Dad's tutoring.

The school insisted that the Smiths take their son to a specialist to get a diagnosis of what kept him from reading, writing, and spelling.

He remembered being hooked up to some wires and drinking some kind of stuff that put him to sleep, but they could find no problems and officially designated that Rickie had a 'learning disability.' He was put into special education classes but still only made Ds and Fs. However, the school always passed him to the next grade. (As an adult, it was determined that Rickie has dyslexia and doesn't see words and letters like most people do. But most schools weren't set up to deal with such problems, or even be aware of them, in those days.)

Rickie made a friend at school and one day talked him into coming home with him after classes. When Red got home and saw the friend, he told him it was time to go home. Then he took Rickie into his room and spanked him.

"Don't you ever bring colored people to our house, again. They have their place and we have ours, but we don't mix."

That upset Rickie very much. Besides that, it was confusing because Red's right-hand man at work was a black man who sometimes went out drinking with him and was a friend in other ways.

One of the times Rickie got into trouble at school, Red told him, "You're just no good. You'll never amount to anything. You are not my son—you're from bad blood. Someday you'll go to prison and they'll sure enough make you mind."

So the eight-year-old boy got Tippy, his dog, and ran away. He went to a former Southern Pacific Railroad Building where hides were treated for leather. He crawled into a bin of salt and went to sleep. Later, a black man who worked there woke him up.

"What do you think you're doing?"

"I'm sleeping. I ran away from home."

"Well, get out of there. You can come home with me."

"Tippy has to go, too."

"Naw, he'll find his way home."

"Then I ain't going, either."

"Well, OK, come on."

Rickie was scared but went with him. Tippy never liked black people, but he got along with this man and even let him pet him. The man fixed chili for supper. He fed Tippy, too.

Rickie and the dog slept on the couch. In the morning, the man asked about home.

"My dad don't want me there. He says I'm no good."

"What about your momma?"

"She loves me."

"Well, you can't stay here, unless you call her and tell her you're OK."

So, Rickie called and Selestia told him to come home. She talked to the man and they agreed to meet at a store nearby.

Red was glad Rickie came home, too. But over and over when Rickie got into trouble or couldn't spell the assigned words, Red would get mad and say hurtful things—often referring to Rickie being adopted. Other times they would do things together and Red would teach his son fishing and working on the house. Rickie knew that deep down his dad loved him, but he expected a lot and Rickie could never measure up.

Rickie was constantly distressed that his folks couldn't get along. He never understood how they could go out at night so happy and come home fighting. He seemed to be in the middle of many of their conflicts. Red not only whipped Rickie over his schoolwork, but also when he didn't work good enough.

Red would carry off lumber from his job—new and used—and he would put Rickie to work pulling nails and cleaning it up. When he did as Red wanted, he would be paid and when he didn't, he was beaten—with a belt or a garden hose or whatever was handy. Selestia tried to intervene and the fight shifted to them, oftentimes getting physical. That hurt Rickie as much as taking the beating himself.

The family moved out of the big metropolitan area of Houston near a community called Liverpool. There, Rickie had access to woods and a bayou where he learned to hunt, trap, and fish. He and Tippy would spend hours in the woods. His folks would have to come and find him to eat or go to bed. He would skip school sometimes and spend all day in the woods. He had a big inner tube and a washtub he would use for boats and sometimes camp out in the woods. He loved the peace of being alone with just Tippy to talk to. They learned to live off the land for a day or more at a time.

T. R. and Selestia were having more and more problems. Rickie felt like most of them were over him. The more he could stay away, the happier he was. The other major issue between his parents was Red's infidelity. Selestia began refusing to go out with him and be the old "Torchy" so he frequently had other female companionship. Red stayed away from home more and more. Even so, they would often make up and try to make a go of it, but quickly would be fighting again. Rickie took his mother's side in the arguments and sometimes even stood up to Red, getting between them.

During this time, the Smiths became friends with Bob and Marcella Thompson. Red met Bob at the bay where Bob had a shrimp boat and barge. The Thompsons had divorced but were now getting remarried to each other. The Smiths went over to wish the Thompsons well. Torchy and Marcella became good friends. They found common ground—party animal husbands.

Rickie went out on Bob's shrimp boat even as a youngster and Bob became a better father figure than Red. While divorced, Marcella had managed a ranch for a wealthy Houston man. When he died, she leased the land and bought the cattle from the widow. So, sometimes the couples would get together at the ranch. Rickie and the Thompsons' daughter, Jodie, were buddies even though she was younger.

Marcella was distressed when the men would catch a calf and put Rickie on it to ride. Naturally, he would get thrown off and sometimes hurt. Red would pick him up, not to console but to put him back on. Whenever Rickie balked, Red would say, "Come on, you sissy." Torchy would try to intervene which just caused more conflict.

Other times, their parties were on Chocolate Bayou. Red had a boat and Rickie was waterskiing by the time he was in school. Marcella wondered sometimes if Red was trying to kill Rickie. He drove the boat too fast and she marveled that Rickie didn't break his neck when he fell. Red would wheel around, pick him up, and get him back on the skis. One time, Rickie fell and started screaming. Red turned around and got him.

"What's the matter with you? You shouldn't be crying—there's no use of that."

Rickie had tumbled into a giant Portuguese man-of-war jellyfish and his body was covered with stings. Eventually, Red realized what had happened and he actually apologized.

Marcella saw Rickie as a good kid, obedient, and well behaved. Like most boys, he tried hard to please his dad but never really could.

The Smiths' marriage continued like a yoyo for years, fueled mostly by Rickie's school problems and Red's partying and affairs. When Rickie was about eleven, Selestia found out about a woman Red was seeing and said she has had enough. T. R. took a job on a building in Baton Rouge, Louisiana, leaving Selestia and Rickie behind.

Marcella talked a lot about Jesus and Selestia decided that church might help get her life straightened out. She and Rickie went with Marcella to Chocolate Bayou Baptist Church. They attended for a while and Rickie went to Vacation Bible School. In one service, Selestia went forward at the altar call to give her heart to Jesus. Rickie went, too. The pastor prayed with them both and soon they were baptized together. But Rickie was really just trying to support his mom because she was so unhappy. They continued to go to church with Marcella and Selestia felt that life was getting better for her. Rickie made some friends and would sit on the back row with them, talking, writing notes, and acting like most kids do in church, but never seemed to get anything from the messages. He gave up trying to sing because he didn't know the songs and couldn't read the words in the hymn book.

By the time T. R. finished the job in Baton Rouge, he and Selestia decided to make a serious effort to put their marriage back together. T. R. even agreed to go to church—a promise he kept three or four times. His plan for being a good husband and dad was to provide their dream house. He bought a place on Chocolate Bayou and began to fix it up and add on to it. He put rock on the outside, remodeled the inside, and built a special room for Rickie and a back porch that had a walkway out to a deck on top of a boathouse on the bayou. It took about a year to get it ready and they moved into it. Rickie loved it. He could swim, fish, hunt—all the things he enjoyed. The family was doing better, too, perhaps because T. R. spent a lot of his off time working on the house.

While the house was good for the family, it also was a great place for parties. The deck became the gathering place for Red's party friends, and pretty soon the turmoil returned. Rickie's problems at school got worse with every grade level, contributing to conflict at home. Besides the difficulty with schoolwork and teachers, he got into arguments and fights with kids. Late in the seventh grade he was in a big fight. He was to be expelled from school, unless he came in every morning and get two licks with the paddle from the principal. After a couple of days Rickie said, "That's it. I won't take anymore," and he left, never to go back. He was passed to the eighth grade but never attended. Often when it was time to go catch the school bus, he would double back, get his row boat, and go down Chocolate Bayou fishing, exploring, and enjoying the day by himself and Tippy.

Naturally, truancy got Rickie into more trouble. Also, Red and Torchy were near the breaking point in their relationship. Rickie's primary focus in going to church had been to get God to fix his home. He earnestly prayed for the Lord to change his dad, help his mom, and make him be able to get along in school. One day, his parents had an especially bad fight. Torchy hit Red with a pan. Rickie knew it was all over. He ran out into the rain, across the street, into the woods, and cried and yelled. This thirteen-year-old boy looked up through the rain and the tall pine trees and cursed God. He listed the things he had asked the Lord to help with and how instead things just got worse. Then he shook his fist towards the sky and yelled, "If that's the kind of God you are, then I don't want anything to do with you!"

CHAPTER THREE

"Come out here!" Red Smith yelled as he beat on the door with both fists, "Unlock this door or I'll bust it down!" It was after midnight and Red just came in from an evening of drinking, planning to climb into bed with Torchy. She knew the routine and already decided she would never go to bed with her husband again. Rickie put her in his room with the door locked. "You belong over here with me," Red shouted as he prepared to break through the door.

Rickie stepped in front of the door ready for the fight. "I ain't going to let you in there." A year or so ago, Rickie had told his dad that he was too old to be whipped with the belt. T. R. took Rickie at his word and changed to using his fists instead. But this time, for some reason, he backed off and the crisis was over.

So was the marriage. Selestia and Rickie moved to a small house a few miles away. Rickie Smith's life took a drastic turn, going from bad to worse, seemingly headed as Red had warned years before. Was it the harsh discipline from his dad? Could it be following the negative examples from his dad? Maybe it was the anger at God for not fixing the problems in his life. Perhaps it was normal teenage rebellion, encouraged by wrong friends. How about too much idle time as a school dropout? Or, probably, all the above?

No longer content to hang out fishing or in the woods, Rickie began stealing things he wanted, then burglarizing houses for money and valuables. He was drinking and smoking. He learned to use wild grapes to make wine in a 5-gallon water jug. He had two buddies—partners in crime. They sniffed paint and gasoline to get high and before long were smoking marijuana and using LSD.

Rickie was fourteen when the divorce happened. That summer he got a job at Luke's Marina, shrimping. He lived on a bait barge 10 miles out in the bay. Although divorced, Selestia and T. R. went together in his boat to the barge—each one telling Rickie to come live with them. The divorce decree said Rickie will live with his mother and he called that home, but he came and went as he pleased. School officials gave Selestia a hard time about Rickie not being in school, but it made no difference to him. He was not about to go back to such "an awful place."

Rickie hung around Luke's Marina on Chocolate Bay. Luke was confined to a wheelchair and had a guy named Ted as his mechanic and all-around helper. Rickie would help Ted, learning many things from him about boats and motors. Ted gave Rickie a 1954 35-horsepower Johnson motor that was collecting dust in the shop—a reward for cleaning up and helping. He and Rickie rebuilt the motor. Rickie worked in exchange for the parts he needed. Someone also gave him an old 15-foot boat with a big hole in its bottom. A friend with a tractor hauled it to the house where Rickie lived with his mom.

T. R. stopped by and saw his son trying to patch the hole and knew he didn't know how, so he helped him to fix it right. So Rickie had his own rig and began fishing and running crab traps. He would pull a shrimp net, gather the shrimp, and use the trash fish as bait in the crab traps. He sold to restaurants and anyone else he could.

A woman named Rose became his best customer, buying shrimp and crabs for the bar and restaurant where she worked. Rose and her daughter Cindy had recently moved into a trailer house in the Liverpool area. Their move from Houston was prompted by a divorce. Rickie and Cindy got acquainted and quickly became more than friends.

Rose let Rickie stay in their home, but she pulled a pistol from her purse, pointed it toward Rickie, and said, "I'll use this on you if I catch you sleeping with my daughter in my house." Then she took Cindy to the doctor and got birth control pills for her. Rickie took the important part of the threat to be "in my house" so their relationship continued hot and heavy, elsewhere.

Sheriff investigators eventually figured out that Rickie was involved in the burglary epidemic in Brazoria County and picked him up for questioning. He and Cindy decided it was time to disappear, to Corpus Christi. They packed a duffel bag and the little bit of money Rickie had made. They hitchhiked into Houston and got on US Highway 90 headed west. In the late 60s, hitchhiking was quite normal. The fifteen-year-old couple got a ride quickly, with a man by himself. He had slicked-down hair, sunglasses, and covered with tattoos. His car was a green 1959 Chevrolet. He stopped and bought hamburgers for all three of them. They told him they were going to Corpus and he said he was going as far as Victoria.

As they were going into Victoria, the driver said he had to go to his mother's house and check on her and if they wanted to go with him, then he could take them on to Corpus Christi. Rickie and Cindy thought that was their good fortune. They went through Victoria and then he pulled off to the shoulder saying a tire must have picked up a nail or something. Then he turned, crossing a cattle guard, and stopped on a gravel driveway so he could change the tire. The tire was flat, but pulling into a field didn't make sense to Rickie and he began to have a funny feeling. While helping with the tire, he stuck a small pipe wrench into his pants. When they got back into the car, the driver went further on the gravel road into some woods and around a curve, turned the car around, and stopped out of sight of the highway.

"What's the deal?" Rickie asked.

The driver replied, "You got three guesses," and he looked at Cindy, sitting between him and Rickie in the front seat. She started cussing the guy out, but Rickie told her to shut up. She looked at Rickie with eyes like daggers, but was quiet. The driver pulled a knife and held it to Cindy's throat, saying, "She is going to do what I tell her to do."

He looked at Rickie who told Cindy, "Just do what he says."

The tattooed man said, "I don't want to have sex with her. I want her to get out of the car and go over by that tree lying on the ground right over there. Then take all her clothes off."

Rickie had to get out to let Cindy out of the car and he quietly told her, "Everything's going to be OK if you just do what he says."

She walked to the dead tree and Rickie sat down on the front seat with his feet out on the ground. The driver had come around the car and looked at Rickie who just kind of hung his head. The guy smiled and with the knife in his hand, started to walk towards Cindy. Rickie knew he would have to be quick and he would have only one chance. The man's attention was on Cindy who was naked by now. Rickie pulled out the wrench as he stood and lunged two steps, swinging the wrench with both hands because it had to be a knockout blow. The wrench made a solid hit on the back of the head and the man fell like a sack of rocks—out cold.

Rickie ran and grabbed Cindy's arm, "Come on, let's go."

"Let me put some clothes on," she said.

"No, just run with me. We've got to get away from here." He scooped up her clothes, grabbed her hand, and started, nearly dragging her down the dirt road to the highway, scared to death. Cindy managed to get some clothes on and they stuck out their thumbs. The third car stopped and they jumped in the backseat. A middle-aged couple were in the front. As they pulled onto the highway, Rickie saw the "pee green" Chevy coming out of the woods, speeding down the dirt road.

"What's wrong?" the lady asked.

"Nothing," Rickie said.

"Are you sure?" the man said, glancing over his shoulder.

Cindy joined Rickie in assuring them they were OK, but it didn't convince the couple.

"Where you going?"

"Home—in Corpus Christi," Rickie said.

Soon, as they were driving into town, the lady asked, "Where do you live in Corpus?"

Rickie kept looking for a sign with a street name. He finally got them to stop and let them out. The couple knew they were lying and something was wrong. As Rickie and Cindy got out, the lady said, "It's dangerous out on the streets. Won't you tell us what's going on?"

"No!" Rickie said and shut the door. They walked away so the nice couple drove off. Rickie stuck out his thumb as other cars came by. Soon one stopped and gave them a ride to the beach on Padre Island.

It was a warm spring evening and the beach was busy. Clumps of people were enjoying varying kinds of fun. Rickie and Cindy blended in with a bunch of party folks for a while. Soon they hitched a ride on down the beach to another party and joined it. Most of the people seemed to be hippies and glad to meet whoever came along. This was 1969, the height of the hippie movement, and Padre Island was a favorite hangout for them. Rickie and Cindy fitted right in.

They hitched a ride intending to go sample the fun with some other group. It was a flowered van driven by James. He had two women with him, one quite young like Rickie and Cindy. The other, Mary, was James' girlfriend, and they were probably in their thirties. James sized up Rickie and Cindy and decided they needed a big brother. They told him they just left home with each other.

"How you going to make a living?" James pressed Rickie.

"We'll get jobs," he said, like anyone with any sense would know that—then asked, "What do you do for a living?"

James didn't reply but headed on into town. He said they could come home with him and the two ladies.

"OK."

James pulled the van into the driveway of a three-bedroom house in a nice neighborhood of Corpus Christi. Mary showed Cindy to the bedroom where she and Rickie would stay. James took Rickie into his bedroom to reveal the answer to the question "What do you do for a living?"

"You can stay here as long as you like, but you cannot tell anyone that you are here. You are not to call anyone back home to tell them where you are."

Rickie said, "No problem."

James opened a walk-in closet door, revealing bricks of marijuana stacked nearly to the ceiling. "I sell drugs," he stated matter-of-factly. "People will be coming to the house to buy at all hours of the day and night. I'll be here most of the time to take care of business and Mary will handle it if I'm gone. Most orders are prepared ahead of time, ready to be picked up."

Rickie found this interesting and exciting, not threatening. He knew it was wrong but didn't care. Cindy was OK with it also. They settled into the house and the "family." Sometimes, Rickie and Cindy would be the only ones home when a buyer came. They would give them the grocery sack with their name on it and the buyer would leave the money. There was always a large pie pan of marijuana in the house for "the family" to use whenever they wanted. Rickie and Cindy smoked their share.

Occasionally, all five of them would sit on the floor with newspapers spread out and fill capsules with powdered mescaline—made from the peyote cactus. Jars of it were kept in the refrigerator. Rickie and Cindy would lick the powder off their fingers. James laughed, "You have to watch and not get too much of this."

On one occasion Cindy did have too much. She began acting crazy and then the trip went bad. She was frantic about the guy who had picked them up and planned to rape her. Rickie tried to calm her down and she went nuts at him, screaming, "Get away from me!"

James tried his hand at calming her, but she decided he was going to rape her. She flailed around and broke a window, cutting her arm. Mary and the young woman also tried to help Cindy. They got her into the car and James drove around and around with the windows down, trying to get her as much fresh air as possible.

Cindy kept crying, "I want to go home."

Finally, in exasperation, Rickie said, "OK, I'll get you back home—just calm down, please."

She listened to Rickie, so James joined in, "I'll take you home, Cindy, I'll take you home."

And he did. That very afternoon, James took Rickie and Cindy all the way to Liverpool, south of Houston, to her mom's trailer house. Rose was glad to see her daughter, but she was very angry. She chewed them out thoroughly for running away and especially for being gone more than a month without a word to her about where they were. Then she called Rickie's mother to come and get him out of her house. Selestia came and Rickie went home with her. Selestia was upset about the kids being gone, too, but even more she was glad her "sweet little Rickie" was back home.

CHAPTER FOUR

Rickie lived with his mom and picked up where he had left off when he and Cindy ran away. He went out early each day fishing, to make money. He also went back to his other job—stealing and breaking into houses around Chocolate Bay.

The sheriff also picked up where he left off when Rickie Smith disappeared and soon Rickie was introduced to what would eventually become home more than anywhere else—jail. While his lifestyle grew into a perplexing mixture of good and evil, the legal system played an almost comical role that allowed, or even encouraged, lawlessness as much as interfering with it.

Rickie still used Luke's Marina as his base for selling fish, shrimp, crabs, and even some oysters. One afternoon, two sheriff's deputies came to arrest him. They put him in handcuffs and took him to the old county jail in Angleton, the Brazoria County Seat.

Two detectives questioned him—using the good cop/bad cop technique. One would tell him how much trouble he was in, then the other would offer to help him if he cooperated. They had a list of thirty-some burglaries and claimed an eyewitness saw him go in his boat to some houses on the bay. Rickie admitted three of the break-ins and denied all the others. He spent that night in a cell by himself. It had steel straps rather than bars. Officers would take other prisoners past his cell, apparently trying to scare him with the prospects he faced, and it worked.

His mom and Cindy came the next day to get him out, in Selestia's custody. She took him to the law office of Mike and Jimmy Phillips— brothers. Mike explained the situation. The charges are in juvenile court and the officials do not want Rickie in that area anymore. The natural result would be to send him to reform school in Gatesville, about 150 miles away, unless they could come up with a good alternative.

Mike ruled out probation because, he said, he knew Rickie would just violate it. He ruled out going into the army because he was only fifteen. So, he proposed that Rickie and Cindy get married and move out of the county. Rickie agreed. They went to a small wedding chapel on Interstate 45 and got married with their parents' approval. Then, in a rather informal court hearing, Rickie pleaded guilty to felony theft and got a ten-day sentence. He also got a tongue lashing from the judge, "This is your only chance, young man. Being married means from now on you would go into district court as an adult. Your free rides are all used up." He narrowed his eyes and lowered, but intensified, his voice, "I better not see you in my court again. You better not even get a traffic ticket here." Then raising his voice, "In fact, you better not even be found in this county." He then pronounced the sentence of ten days in the county jail, but permitted him to serve it in three weekends.

In jail, Rickie met Sheriff Robert Gladney, a huge man. He wore custom-made cowboy boots with a big G inlaid in the tops. He kept several pair at the courthouse and Rickie was assigned to shine them. Sheriff Gladney carried an axe handle when he made rounds through the jail. Besides being sheriff, he owned a chain of grocery stores and some shrimp boats. Some prisoners said they got extra good time credit off their sentences by working on Gladney's shrimp boats.

Anyhow, Rickie was introduced to jail and a rather freewheeling justice system at the early age of fifteen. Also, the judge, attorneys, sheriff, and families could all claim they had dealt with the problem of Rickie Smith's criminal career.

Contrary to his earlier declarations of abandoning Rickie if he went to jail, T. R. Smith stepped up to help his son significantly. He got Rickie into Carpenter Union #213 as an apprentice and a job on a construction project in Houston—building Buffalo Towers. He also signed the note for a loan to buy a house trailer for the new couple to live in, just outside the city. He even came and helped hook up the utilities. He co-signed for a new Ford Maverick.

Selestia signed the note for Rickie to buy a motorcycle. She and Rose, Cindy's mother, contributed items needed to set up housekeeping.

So, the collusion of parents, court and attorney resulted in two very immature kids, with limited education, getting married and beginning a new life together.

Rickie was determined to succeed. He even took a second job on an oil rig just down the road from their house so he could be a good provider and deal with the debts. Working two shifts a day left Cindy alone most of the time, out in the country and bored. When Rickie had days off, they would make up for lost time with drugs and alcohol. Soon the marriage was slipping downhill. It didn't help that Cindy's mom would come and get her, frequently, and that her brother decided their trailer was a good place to hang out—and do drugs.

One night the couple went to the beach at Freeport, although it was legally off-limits for Rickie. Coming back, Rickie was passed out on "Reds" (drugs) and beer so Cindy drove. Rickie woke up in the little pile of wreckage that was left of the Maverick with blood all over him. Someone had called an ambulance and the highway patrol. Cindy was badly injured and Rickie had a gash on his head. They were put into the ambulance and headed for the hospital. Cindy kept saying, "I'm sorry, Rickie, I'm sorry."

He reassured her, "It's OK, don't worry about it now."

She said, "I'm so very sorry."

"It's all right. Things just happen sometimes."

"No," Cindy said, "I was trying to kill us with that bridge."

"What?" Rickie yelled.

"I'm sorry, Rickie."

His gut reaction was to throw her out of the ambulance; to keep from doing that, he turned away for the rest of the trip.

Cindy was in the hospital over a week with a ruptured spleen, broken ribs, and bruises. Rickie was treated and released.

The Maverick was hauled from the scene in two pieces. The insurance paid it off. Cindy got a ticket for speeding. After the wreck, things went even worse between Rickie and Cindy, and came to a head very soon. Early one morning, Rickie came in from the oil rig to take a bath, eat, and go to the construction job. The living room floor looked like a drugstore and Cindy and her brother were high, shooting speed. Rickie and the brother got into a fight and Rickie ran him off. Then he and Cindy had a big fight. Rose came to get Cindy and Rickie told her, "Get her out of here and just keep her—she's yours, not mine, anymore." The marriage had lasted about a year, an extremely turbulent year, and they divorced.

Rickie quit the oil field job but worked hard as a carpenter, advancing from an apprentice to a journeyman, even though he was only seventeen. But of course he also diligently pursued his other life—drugs, alcohol, sex, and fighting. It seemed there was always a fight to get into. Rickie was tough—a good fighter. Some fights were his own doing but many were on behalf of "friends." People figured out that Rickie could be finagled into fighting for them—not only to avoid fighting themselves but also because if Rickie did it for them, they would most likely win. Rickie's usual "cocktails" during this time were "speed," "black mollies," and whiskey.

He rented the house trailer for $20 more than the monthly payments and went to live with his dad in the Telephone Road Apartments in south Houston. They couldn't get along, so Rickie got his own apartment.

One evening, Rickie went to the McClendon Triple outdoor theater, on Telephone Road near Pearland, just outside Houston. He met Donna. She was some years older. She managed a barbecue place in the Alameda Mall. She liked to party and hit it off very well with Rickie. Soon, they got married—a couple of months after his first marriage ended. They lived in an apartment complex on Interstate 45, in south Houston. Cindy knew where it was and would come over frequently, trying to get Rickie back. Obviously that caused trouble for both Rickie and Donna.

Eventually, they moved into a two-story apartment in Sharpstown, an upscale area of Houston. Rickie acquired a 55 Chevy and made it into a real hot rod, besides a Honda he owned.

A young teenager, named Tim, lived nearby and hung around watching Rickie work on souping up the Chevy. He seemed to always be high on something, although Rickie never shared any drugs or alcohol with him. One evening, Tim came and Donna let him in. He was so spaced out on marijuana he could hardly talk. Pretty soon he left through the back door. His mother saw him and could tell he was on something so she called the police. They got a warrant and came to the apartment. Rickie recognized the police knock on the front door, so he grabbed his one pound sack of marijuana and ran out the back. A cop ambushed him and threw him on the trunk of his car, scattering weed everywhere. Rickie was arrested for drug possession and taken to jail where he was stuck for a couple of weeks. His attorney was able to get the charges dropped by convincing the prosecutors that the police had a faulty search warrant. That was the beginning of a long succession of arrests for drugs, concealed weapons, and assault.

Rickie progressed as a carpenter and was now working as a form carpenter on the new high-rise Telephone Building. He was making $14.00 an hour, very good money in 1972. He seemed to be following in his dad's footsteps, career-wise, and partying. One day Rickie came home, having been gone for two days. Donna had reached her limit and confronted him. They had a big fight. She started throwing things and breaking stuff in the apartment. He went upstairs to get some clothes and came down to leave. Donna started hitting him, so he pushed her down and left. But out on the sidewalk she came running up behind him. He turned around and slugged her, knocking her cold. He loaded his car and left.

When he was gone, a woman named Becky came by with her boyfriend, Ozzie, and found Donna unconscious. They called an ambulance for her. Several days later, Donna's little sister called Rickie. She asked him for some marijuana and said, "Come over and pick me up. I have something you'll want to know about."

He went. He gave her some "weed" then asked, "OK what is it?"

She said, "Donna is over at Tony's place. I figured you'd like to know." Tony was a good friend of Rickie's.

He immediately went to Tony's apartment and kicked in the door. Tony and Donna were in bed on a hide-a-bed in the living room. Rickie grabbed a lamp with a marble base and beat Tony with it until he was unconscious. Donna had grabbed a sheet and run into the bathroom, locking the door. Rickie got a butcher knife from a kitchen drawer and yelled, "You're next, Donna. Come out of there!" Naturally, she stayed. He stabbed the knife through the door, then kicked it in. "That knife was just to scare you," he said, and let her run out of the apartment naked. Then he gathered up her clothes and Tony's stereo, took them out, and threw them into the swimming pool. That was the end of their relationship, although they didn't officially divorce until years later.

Soon after that, Rickie was with a girl named Peggie, drinking beer at her apartment. Becky knew Peggie and came by to chat. The conversation got around to Becky finding this woman unconscious on the sidewalk and added, "She was beaten by some sorry #@&!$#." Peggie started making faces and motions to alert Becky that she was talking about Rickie.

"I'm that sorry #@&!$# that knocked his wife out," he said.

Becky turned red and ran to the bathroom as Rickie laughed.

When Becky came out and left, Rickie followed her, asking her to go out with him.

"Do you want to knock me out, too?" she asked.

His response was a sexual comment. He kept after her and finally she accepted. Their first time for sex was on Christmas Day, his nineteenth birthday. Very soon Rickie moved in with her. Becky had two children and Rickie was good with them. He became a substitute dad. He seemed to be the kind of dad he had wished for years earlier.

Rickie and Becky had a turbulent relationship for a couple of years. There were drugs, bars, fights, jail, disagreements with each other, and friends as bad as or worse than they were. Amazingly, Rickie kept working. If he was in jail too long to go back to a job, he'd find another construction site and get a new job, as long as he kept up with his union dues. And he knew his dad's name and reputation helped when he needed to use it. Houston was booming and construction was a major industry. Also, many carpenters were known for not showing up for work from time to time, so work and good pay were always available.

Most arrests meant a day or two in jail and then released. Sometimes he had to post bond to get out, but formal charges were never pursued or, in a few instances, would be settled for "time served"—in instances where Rickie had stayed in jail a couple of weeks or so. At least twice, he "jumped bail" forfeiting the posted bond and hoping to not get caught again in that jurisdiction. Wherever Rickie went, people seemed to really like him, whether they were party friends, other jail-birds, policemen, construction workers, or incidental brief acquaintances.

About six months into their relationship, Rickie and Becky went to a Summer Jam at Charlotte Speedway in North Carolina. There were thirty-seven rock bands jamming for three days. Becky's sister went with them. It was in June 1974. Drugs were everywhere and most everyone was high or worse. Even before it started, the mass of people pushed down the fence around the place. The police brought in reinforcements and apparently decided to just keep order outside and leave people alone inside—as long as they stayed inside. Revelers resented the high prices for food, water, and other concessions so the booths and trucks were overrun and some even burned—the first day—so there was nothing to eat or drink the other two days.

The second day, Rickie went to the car to get something and was arrested as he stepped outside. He naturally protested and resisted so he got beaten up, then put on a bus and hauled to jail. A day or so later, Becky came to post bond—with a $600 hot check and they left town.

Not long afterward, Rickie's mother decided to go to Anaheim,

California, to care for her father who was dying of cancer. He and Becky loaded Selestia into their 1973 Malibu and drove to the West Coast. They decided to stay and settled in Costa Mesa. This set up one of the more interesting of a long string of arrests over several years. Rickie was pretty well spaced out on barbiturates and alcohol—a deadly mix—and he side-swiped a parked car in Newport Beach. He kept going planning to get away, but it was on a peninsula and he turned and was coming back only a block over from the wreck. The police spotted him and stopped him. As he "rolled" out of the car, the bottle of pills fell over in his lap and scattered on the ground and the officer's foot.

He was booked into the Orange County Jail, known as the "Glass House" to sleep off the drugs. The next day he was arraigned in court and bond was set at $500. However, they released him on his own recognizance and allowed to leave with the promise that he would return for the next court hearing. The judge said that if he would get the car he hit fixed, he would consider dropping the charges.

He was in such a hurry to leave he didn't call Becky and he had no money to get home. He was walking across the street when Selestia drove by in her dad's car, saw him, and stopped. She was coming to visit them in their apartment and got lost. Rickie jumped in, "How did you know I was in jail, Mom?"

"Jail? Son, I'm lost, trying to find you and Becky." Selestia decided that God had intervened and Rickie thought that had to be the case, too. It shook him up, but within a few days he was back on drugs. The car he hit was small and he totaled it. They wanted $2,000. Rickie fixed his car and they packed up and went back to Houston, and ignored the matter.

Back in Houston meant working in construction. He worked for a dry-wall company a few times. The requirement was that two men had to hang eighty sheets in a day. Rickie had no problem meeting the quota. Becky also had good jobs as a legal secretary.

Another highlight in the numerous jail experiences occurred in Atlanta, Georgia, in 1975. Rickie was known so well to police in and all around Houston, he and Becky decided to go to Atlanta where her dad was vice president of a bank. She immediately got a job in a law firm, but Rickie was unemployed. Becky's car was in the shop one day so she borrowed a car from her dad. Ricky took her to work then picked up a friend who brought his girlfriend and a girl friend of hers. They went to Piedmont Park and hung out smoking pot and snorting cocaine. At noontime they were driving around and passed by an outdoor restaurant where Becky, some lawyers, and others from the firm were having lunch. Becky saw the car go by and assumed Rickie was hooked up with the extra girl, so she called her dad who called the police to report his car stolen. Later, Rickie went to the house to get Becky, but her daughter said she had left with her dad, "and you better go away because the cops are looking for you."

Rickie stashed the dope he had. "Where is your mom?"

"At the Twenty-Seven Birds." It's a nightclub that Rickie knew, so he headed over there, still in the dad's car.

Becky was sitting in a booth with a man.

Why the heck did you call the laws on me? He demanded.

The man stood up to say something, but Rickie knocked him out cold. The bouncers jumped on Rickie and held him until the police arrived. He was put in Fulton County Jail. Prisoners were allowed to keep the change in their pocket to use in a pay phone, so he stuck in a quarter and dialed the operator. His quarter dropped into the coin return and immediately a black man reached in and grabbed it. Rickie started fighting with him and the other prisoners—all black—jumped him. The guards came and dragged him out by the feet with the other prisoners still stomping on him. He was taken to a solitary cell, bloody, swollen, and hurting.

He remembered what his dad had always told him, "Black people need to stay in their places and white people need to stay in theirs." That was beginning to make more sense now. So, in a couple of days, when he was taken to meet his court-appointed attorney and saw that he was black, he went ballistic and called the lawyer every racial slur he could think of. He kicked the Plexiglas that was between them, wanting to get to the man, but it didn't break. The attorney sat calmly, watching this tirade, then asked "Are you through?" Rickie threw out a few more names, then just looked at him.

"You have called me a lot of names and things, but the one thing you didn't call me is 'a good attorney' and that's something you're in need of right now. That is, if you want to get out of here." Rickie stared at the lawyer, thought it over, and sat down to listen. Before the day was over, he learned that what the man said was true. They went to court, facing two attorneys from the bank, sent to make sure Rickie got the maximum sentence for stealing Becky's father's car. The black attorney pointed out how they were part of a setup to railroad Rickie and explained how he and Becky have lived together and she gave him the keys to take her to work. The case was dismissed.

Rickie walked out, caught a bus to Becky's apartment, showed her his two black eyes, and said, "Get a good look at them because you're fixin' to have two just like them." He beat her up, got his drugs and money, took a cab to the airport, and flew to California.

CHAPTER FIVE

Rickie Smith had an aunt Rusty, his mother's sister, in Los Angeles. She had asked him more than once to come and help her, probably because Selestia had expressed deep concern for Rickie and all the trouble he kept getting into. So, when he bailed out of Atlanta he went to Aunt Rusty's. She had some serious health problems and needed help, which she got from Rickie for a few days. But soon he was back with the wrong people doing the wrong things. He met a young woman and, as usual, they hit it off good. He began sleeping at the woman's house and doing cocaine, eating a variety of pills, and drinking with her and her mother.

For two months he stayed high most of the time and became a real mess. Obviously he was no help to Aunt Rusty. She confronted him, telling him he has to get a job and move out of her house. He did neither so she finally bought a plane ticket for him to go back to Houston.

Back in his old town, Rickie went back to his old ways. He got a job remodeling the Shell Oil Company Research Center Building and stayed with some friends. The work went on and on. It seemed strange because they would change walls and cabinets turning an office into a laboratory room then soon they'd change the same room back into an office and sometimes later change it back into a lab again. Sometimes he was hanging sheetrock, other times putting Formica on countertops or framing walls, but he was good at all of it and was paid well. So he was back into his old rhythm, juggling work with drinking, drugs, girls, fighting, and trying to stay out or get out of jail.

One day, Rickie returned to work after several days of partying and jail. While he was in a somewhat more stable routine, he reflected on the turmoil of the previous week and thought, *Man, those people are no good. Their whole life revolves around drugs, sex, fights, stealing, running from the police, hiding from family, tearing up cars, wasting money and all kinds of stuff. Why do I keep hanging around them?* He felt some pride in doing a good job and always being able to get work. He thought about his mother who loved him so much, even when he caused her so much anxiety. He even thought about God and what his mother had said many times about doing what God would be pleased with. He recalled how Marcella Thompson had told him that we must serve the Lord to have a good life. And remembered the hope he felt when he and Selestia were baptized at Chocolate Bayou Baptist Church and said they were committing their lives to God.

But those thoughts soon progressed to telling himself, *Why should I care what God wants? After all, He didn't keep my family together when I begged Him to.* He vividly remembered running away from the fight his parents were having and looking up to the sky through the rain and cursing God because he had paid no attention to the one request Rickie had made of him—to remove the turmoil and put his family together, happy. *Apparently even God doesn't have any reason to care about me. I must be worthless. My mother didn't want me and gave me away, my new dad always told me I would never amount to anything and plenty of other folks agree with him about that. So, I was right in telling God I wanted nothing to do with Him.*

His thoughts came full circle, *These people are my friends. They like me. They want me around. They always invite me to spend the evening or the night with them. If I don't hang out with them, I don't have any friends. They have different values and lifestyles than some people I used to know but I fit in with them and we have lots of fun. My dad and sometimes even Mom partied big time. Besides, who's to say those folks are right and these people are wrong?* So he dismissed the feelings that brought on that string of thoughts.

Life in jails had some similarities to life in general—for Rickie. There was always someone to hassle you and every day presented the choice of shrinking into the background or standing up for yourself. From early childhood Rickie was taught to "be a man" so he wouldn't turn away from any challenge. He was never a bully and it was against his personal code of morals to take advantage of another person, but he seemed to always be surrounded by those who would. So, trouble dogged him.

Increasingly, that trouble involved black men, like the problems in the Atlanta jail. Another example was one time that Rickie was booked into the Harris County Jail in Houston. He had been shooting speed without sleeping for several days and needed to crash. The jail was overcrowded, as usual, and all the bunks were taken, so he picked a spot on the floor and went to sleep. When it came time to count the inmates, everyone is called to the day room to be counted. All that commotion didn't wake him up. But the kicking and stomping by the "floor boys" did. In the 5-5 Tank, the "floor boys" (inmates who are bosses) were black. Rickie was taken to the infirmary and then moved just outside Houston to Harris County Rehab in Humble, Texas. The prisoners there seemed to be the most hardened and difficult ones. At rehab, the inmate bosses were called "hall boys" instead of "floor boys." A black "hall boy" beat Rickie up, but this time he didn't get moved. Somehow, he was able to concoct a bucket full with a mixture of boiling water, syrup, and soap. While the "hall boy" was sleeping, he threw it on him. With help from other "hall boys," Rickie got beaten up again. This time he was moved to a solitary cell.

A Sheriff Department lieutenant named Anderson took notice of white guys who would stand up for themselves. He gave Rickie a job on a paint crew which was housed in an all-white cell block, called "the white house." A few weeks later, Rickie saw one of the "floor boys" who had stomped him back in the county jail coming into the rehab facility. Because of his job, Rickie could move around the place and managed to get into the holding cell of the former "floor boy" and beat him up, ending with some serious stomping. A case was filed against Rickie and he was locked up for this offense, but when he explained to Lt. Anderson that it was a fair fight, one-on-one with no weapons, the case was torn up and Rickie went back to his job with the "white house" crew until he was released.

Those ongoing racial wars kept reminding Rickie of his dad's teaching that blacks should stay in their place, separate from white people. They also helped, years later, to push Rickie into a fateful decision which would dramatically impact his life and help bring on the reputation which was the subject of the hearing in Judge Whitaker's Courtroom, back in chapter one.

Whenever Rickie was in jail more than a couple of days, he would get visits from girlfriends and from Selestia, who never gave up on her "sweet little Rickie." As soon as he got out, he would go to the Carpenters Union Hall and find a new job. Or, if he saw a sign at a job site, he'd stop in and sign on, usually back at Shell Research, where he worked most for over two years. He always kept up his union membership and dues.

During this time, Rickie got acquainted with a pharmacist at Twelve Oaks Towers Pharmacy on Southwest Freeway in Houston. The pharmacist, Timmy Hayes, became a source of all kinds of prescription drugs. When drugs went out of date, instead of disposing of them in the incinerator, he would sell them to Rickie. Also, Timmy would clue Rickie in to doctors who would write prescriptions they could get filled for drugs. Besides using them, Rickie built a thriving business selling the drugs. He would take girls from the topless clubs to do sexual favors for certain doctors in exchange for prescriptions.

There was a young woman in the usual group of party friends that Rickie liked and they hit it off together. Her name was Donna—a different Donna from the one he had married, beat up, and left unconscious but had never divorced. He and this Donna hung out together more and more. She played a key role in the growing drug business. She would dress up in younger girl clothes, fix her hair in pigtails, and flirt with the doctors and get them to write her prescriptions. One older doctor especially enjoyed Donna making eyes at him and sitting in his lap. Donna also became a heavy user of the drugs, along with Rickie. They progressed from popping the pills to mashing them and making solutions to shoot into their veins with hypodermic needles.

Amazingly, even when strung out, Rickie seemed able to keep his wits about him. When some situation arose that required some sound thinking, he could cut through the fog to analyze the circumstances and make decisions on the best way to deal with them. That ability, along with his personal code of honor, had served Rickie well through all of the chaos of his twenty years of life.

Timmy Hayes, the pharmacist, warned Rickie that the police were cracking down and getting closer to them. Soon, they saw some of their friends and customers getting arrested. Rickie told Donna that she had to cut back on using drugs. Her favorite was hydro morphine, nicknamed "D's," that she would shoot in her veins and she wasn't interested in slowing down. Rickie made a plan and told Donna, "The cops are getting closer so we're going to leave town and go to California. You'll have to stop altogether when we leave, so cut back, now."

Telling her that turned out to be a big mistake. That night when Rickie went to sleep, Donna gathered up all the drugs and cash she could find, took his car, and left. The car was a hot rod Rickie had completely rebuilt and souped up. He had spent $3,000 on it, plus lots of stolen parts he traded drugs for.

The next day, Rickie "souped up" himself on speed and, with a drug partner who had a car, spent five days looking for Donna. He'd stick a gun in people's faces demanding to know where she was. He kicked in the doors of several places where he thought she might be hiding. Once he spotted a guy she had been seen with in a pickup truck and chased him on the 610 Interstate Loop around Houston. He shot several holes in the truck before giving up.

Finally, late one afternoon, he spotted her in a phone booth by a Stop-&-Go convenience store. She was having sex with two guys while several others sat on the tailgate of their trucks waiting for their turn in the phone booth. He jumped out of the car with a 12-gauge shotgun, scattering all the men who burned rubber off their tires getting away. Donna ran but he caught her. She threw a milkshake in his face but he grabbed her hair and dragged her to the car. He got her into the backseat and told her to give back whatever is left. Between using, spending, and being robbed, she had very little.

Rickie and the friend took Donna to a secluded spot where Rickie planned to kill her. He had grown into the drug-dealer code that says you cannot let anyone get away with anything. If they can't pay what they owe or if they steal from you, then you have to show that they can't get away with it. Besides, Rickie was revved up on speed and an out-of-control rage. He beat her mercilessly, but the friend stopped him before he killed her. He left her there, tied to a concrete pillar.

A young woman friend of Donna's found her, called an ambulance, and soon the police were involved. After interviewing Donna at the hospital, Houston officers issued warrants to arrest Rickie Smith for kidnapping and assault. They issued bulletins to all law enforcement agencies, making this a much more serious issue than the countless run-ins Rickie had before. There are many other charges waiting for his arrest as Donna had given detectives a thorough description of the life and drug business she had shared with him.

Rickie and Donna had shared an apartment, and frequently other people shared it, too. Because of that, he kept a private apartment separate from his official address, so he could get away and not worry about the drug business or the law. As an additional security precaution, Rickie frequently stayed in motels so there could be no connection to his apartments. Money was no problem with the drug business booming. He always had thousands of dollars in his pockets. Donna knew all those details and in her severely injured condition, she gave the information to police. They immediately searched and staked out both apartments and began frequenting all the bars, clubs, and motels Rickie used for business and pleasure. That cat and mouse game went on for two weeks.

Rickie stayed scarce—mostly holed up in motels with a new friend named Marlee. One evening he sent her out to the car to get some pills.

Police had surrounded the motel and they grabbed Marlee. When she didn't return, Rickie sensed there was trouble. He cautiously looked out and decided his only hope was to make a run for it. He bolted out the door and took off for the stairs as fast as he could. There he was met by officers. Between the cops and the stairs, Rickie was battered, handcuffed, and stuffed into a patrol car.

Authorities barely got Rickie settled into the Harris County Jail when Donna came to them to say that she made up all that stuff about Rickie and that she will not testify against him—even on the assault charges. Not that anyone so heavily addicted to drugs could be a credible witness, anyway. So the police were scrambling to build a case against Rickie. The heat that caused him to try to rein in Donna was becoming a major criminal investigation. It took a lot of detailed detective work and analyzing paper trails. Eventually, the pharmacist and at least one doctor went to prison for all the fake prescriptions that had been used, allowing drugs into the hands of street dealers. It was treated as an organized crime prosecution involving up to 350 possible defendants. Even though Rickie had been in the middle of it all, they were having trouble officially connecting him. But he was stuck in the Harris County Jail well over a year. Finally, prosecutors gave up on more serious charges and Rickie was to be tried for possession of a controlled substance, since he did have lots of pills in his car when arrested. He ended up with a conviction and was introduced to the Texas Department of Corrections (TDC) to serve up to twenty years.

A few months into that prison term, he was returned to Houston to be arraigned on a charge of "armed robbery of a donut shop." Never mind that Rickie had never been in that place and the illogic that a man with over three thousand dollars in his pocket when arrested would hold up a small donut shop for a few dollars. But they put together a very convincing case and had Rickie facing more time in prison. He decided to negotiate which resulted in a ten-year sentence for a guilty plea for robbing a place he had never seen. The time would be served at the same time as the drug conviction.

When Rickie arrived at TDC, he went to the Diagnostic Unit in

Huntsville, as do all new inmates. After a few weeks of evaluation and indoctrination, he was sent to the Central Unit outside of Sugarland, near Houston. It was one of the oldest Texas prisons, its history tracing back to being a private plantation where prisoners were sent to work the fields in the late 1800s. It became an official prison in 1908.

Prison felt a lot like jail, only more so. *This must be what Hell is like*, Rickie said to himself and to anyone who listened. In mid 1978, Texas prisons were in turmoil. Racial tension was high. Weaker inmates were easy prey for the tough ones. In fact, cell blocks were all run by inmates. Building tenders (BTs) were the official bosses, chosen by the prison administrators and backed by the few guards on staff. The BTs' assignment was to keep order in exchange for special privileges and status within the prison population. There were not nearly enough officers to control the prisons. Besides BTs there were some unofficial bosses— inmates who were tough enough to intimidate others to do favors, whether sex, providing items from their commissary, or doing chores for them. We'll look more deeply into the operation of the prisons and the chaos in the growing system in chapter seven.

Rickie tried to follow the rules and be a good citizen. But he would not be pushed around and he "stood up" to all who tried. He quickly learned that you have to fight or become a homosexual, or worse—"you would be used like a rag." He was challenged and tested many times but always held his own. He preferred to be left alone, but that was not possible among the many predators. His mother visited him often. One time he would have a black eye on one side and the next time the other eye would be swollen and bruised. So, Rickie was a "good citizen" within the routinely violent inmate society—not too much different from his life before prison. Besides violence among inmates, building tenders and even officers used physical force to deal with inmate problems. He sometimes had drugs smuggled in to him or obtained from other convicts. Many other inmates used drugs, too.

Most of his fights were initiated by someone else, but he still got blemishes in his record. The only choice he saw was to become strong and violent or to "go down." Even so, his goal was to stay out of trouble and make parole as soon as possible. Central was a very difficult prison and anyone who stood up for himself could not keep a clean record, so when he came up for parole it was denied. That was a hard pill to swallow and made Rickie more determined to take care of himself, since no one else cared. After three years in the no-win life in Central, he was denied parole again.

To make matters worse, he was transferred to an even tougher prison, the infamous Eastham Prison Farm northeast of Huntsville. Rickie learned immediately that he moved from a bad situation to a terrible one. At his third hearing, he was recommended for parole. But his ray of hope was quickly turned off by Texas Governor William Clements, who vetoed his parole. Clements was the first Republican governor since reconstruction days following the civil war. He ran on a "law and order" platform. Rickie was bitter over the veto of his parole. He smuggled all the drugs he could get through visitors and learned how to manipulate officers to bring him more. He was usually high on drugs and he very deliberately determined that whenever he gets out, "I will take everything back that prison is taking from me." He decided everyone was against him, everything is someone else' fault—the system, guards, inmate snitches, anyone.

Then came a change. Texas prisons were overcrowded (in violation of the federal court order to be explained in chapter 7). So, Rickie was transferred to the prerelease prison unit and in six months he was to be released under a Mandatory Supervision program. That was a way to move out inmates to make room for new ones coming in. In effect, the inmate was supervised in the community rather than taking up a prison bed. However, Rickie refused to accept mandatory supervision and declared that he would stay until he completed his sentence so he would have no obligations. He was already in the process for release and even though he refused to sign any papers, he was discharged from TDC in February 1983 and his first prison term was history. But, alas, his freedom was short-lived.

CHAPTER SIX

There was nothing particularly remarkable about Rickie Smith's five-and-a-half years in prison on drug charges. Yes, there were conflict, violence, and drugs, but that was fairly routine. However, it was a remarkable time for the Texas Department of Corrections. The whole system was in chaos which is why Rickie didn't stand out. In prison, as he always had, he stood up for himself and did not let anyone push him around. But that involved mostly other inmates and he didn't get in much trouble with the officers.

The prisons were severely understaffed and the inmate population growing by leaps and bounds. This was society's era of getting tough on crime and handing out long sentences, even for relatively minor drug offenses and especially in Texas. A lawsuit was in Federal Court which would soon turn the state prisons upside down and we'll look more deeply into that turmoil in the next chapter. For now, suffice it to say that in much of the Texas Department of Corrections, the guards had their hands full and the inmates were almost on their own.

One of the most difficult prisons was the Eastham Unit where Rickie spent a year-and-a-half of his first prison term. One particular incident there started in a cell block but was moved into an office where Rickie, another inmate, and three officers "scuffled" with each other. Apparently, it was just Rickie against a sergeant, a lieutenant, a captain, and the other inmate, a building tender. The captain finally ended the melee with

Rickie crumpled under the desk. That captain was Keith Price. He does not remember that event—there were too many to recall each one—but many years later he would become a key person in Rickie Smith's life.

Keith Price was born in 1951. He grew up in Gatesville, Texas—home to the juvenile prisons of the Texas Youth Council. Many people in town worked at the juvenile prisons but Keith's father was the boss of a road crew with the Texas Highway Department. Keith had a good upbringing with a brother and a sister. He was a boy scout with cousins and an uncle who was a troop leader. He and his brother achieved the rank of Eagle Scout. He lettered in high school football and dabbled in other sports. The family, including grandparents, went to First Baptist Church. At age twelve, Keith followed the "urging of the Spirit" on Easter Sunday to come down from the balcony, "accept the Lord," and be baptized.

While in high school he worked at a supermarket, eventually becoming a butcher. He continued that work while commuting to a nearby town for two years of junior college and saved enough money to pay for his junior year in a university. At Central Texas College, he had become interested in criminal justice courses so he transferred to Sam Houston State in Huntsville, Texas, which had the premier criminal justice degree program. He was planning to be a probation officer. Huntsville is home to the headquarters of the Texas prison system and is surrounded by prison units. Keith got a summer job as a guard in the furniture factory of the Ramsey One Prison Unit. He saved enough money to pay for his senior year and graduate with a bachelor degree in Criminal Justice.

He also got married. His bride had two more years of school so he took a full time job as an officer in the prison system, assigned to the Ellis Unit, north of Huntsville.

Keith's father, who had passed away the year before, had always told his kids that in his work there were people with a good education who worked in air conditioned offices while the others, like him, worked on the road crews. He impressed on them the advantages of education. So, while beginning his job with TDC and starting a family, Keith went into the master's degree program. He actually enjoyed academics and did well.

He also did well in his job. He seemed to understand inmates and most of them responded to him favorably. That, plus the rapid growth of the prisons, helped him make lieutenant at the first opening, after only a year as an officer. With that promotion came a house for his family on the prison grounds at the Eastham Unit, a 30-minute drive from the university. Three-and-a-half years later he was promoted to captain. Meanwhile, he finished the master's degree and began a PhD. It was in that period that he had that encounter in the office with Rickie Smith. For Price it was part of another day at the office, but for Smith it was an ugly memory burned into his mind, probably because he lost to the officers.

Continuing his rapid rise in the prison system, Price's good work paid off and brought him to a career and life-changing move. Soon after that altercation with Rickie in 1982, he became Major Keith Price. In the prison system, a major is under the warden and assistant wardens. His focus is supervising the officers more than dealing with inmates. Keith was adapting well to that when circumstances changed the dynamics of Texas' fight with a federal court.

It was not long after the "scuffle" in Captain Price's office that Rickie went into the process that resulted in early release. He went back to Houston, initially to his mother's house, and quickly got a job through the Carpenters Union. Selestia bought him a new motorcycle and he picked up where he left off six years before. He started with a new girlfriend, Monica. She was a very pretty redhead who actually was "given" to Rickie by Mike, an inmate friend in Jester One, the prerelease unit.

That was another in the long string of bizarre happenings in Rickie Smith's life. It happened like this: Rickie was in the prison visitor's area with Becky, his on-and-off girlfriend. She had come back into his life in spite of the beating he gave her in Atlanta.

Their relationship took many weird turns, such as an incident which occurred a year before prison. They were living together, but Becky had an affair with a man Rickie worked with. So he found a seventeen-year-old girl named Teresa and brought her home.

"Pack your stuff and get out," he told Becky, spinning Teresa around in front of her. "I have a brand-new model. You have 24 hours to move everything out or I'll pile it up in the backyard and burn it. If you're still here, I'll put you in the fire, too."

Becky left. But as usual, it wasn't long before she was back. She was his most frequent visitor while in prison, except for his mother.

So while Becky was visiting at Jester One, Rickie was eyeing Monica. Becky had smuggled marijuana and some pills to Rickie. Mike told Rickie he would give Monica to him if he would promise to bring her to see him when Rickie got out—and bring a bag of marijuana to him.

"You got a deal," Rickie said. He hooked up with her as soon as he got settled in Houston, but it did not last long. She was young and too wild—even for Rickie. She had a heroin habit and was hooked on methadone, too. She was a prostitute by trade and had a bad temper and a loud mouth. The last he saw of her was when he stopped himself from shooting her with a .38 pistol and instead kicked her, literally, out of his truck at one of her customers' house.

Soon, Rickie found a source for prescription drugs and was dealing and using like there was no tomorrow. He began hanging out with his ex-wife, Donna. One evening, Donna had taken their dirty clothes to the Laundromat and saw Rickie sitting on his Harley in a parking lot and talking to Becky who was sitting in her car. Becky frequently came around to see Rickie, so Donna naturally assumed that something was going on between them. She went berserk, gathered up his clothes and a duffel bag that had 20 pounds of marijuana in it. She threw everything at him, scattering clothes and "weed" in the parking lot, and sped off. Then Rickie went berserk too. He gathered up his clothes and the marijuana, pitching them into Becky's car. Then he roared off to Donna's house. He beat her up, got the pistol he kept at her house, stuck it in her mouth, and threatened to shoot. He relented, grabbed a bunch of methamphetamine pills he had hidden there, and took off. He stopped at a biker bar called Scooters. As he simmered down, he got acquainted with a young woman. She got high and drunk and they decided to move their party to her apartment without even learning each other's name. As she got onto the motorcycle behind Rickie, he saw a police car turn on its flashing blue and red lights. The officers were stopping a car with an expired inspection sticker, but Rickie assumed they were after him. He took off as fast as he could, losing his passenger off the motorcycle. She was almost run over by the police who gave chase. Two blocks later, Rickie hit a car and flew through the air. Of course pills also flew everywhere.

Officers took him to an emergency room where it was determined that he had a broken arm, a broken leg and numerous cuts and bruises, but nothing life-threatening. He was patched up and put in two casts under police guard then taken to the infirmary wing of the Harris County Jail where he stayed several months. His freedom had ended at ninety-five days.

Of course, Selestia was extremely distressed but there was absolutely no way for her to help her "sweet little boy" except to visit, frequently. Red Smith, his dad, immediately wrote him off and had nothing to do with him. Of course, Becky showed up. She brought drugs, including heroin, when she came to the jail to visit and they would stuff them into the casts on his arm and leg. Rickie would also take pain medicines from other patients in the hospital tank of the jail.

When the prosecutors built their case for trial, Rickie took a plea bargain deal for possession of a controlled substance. He got a ten-year sentence and headed back to prison. There was also a conviction on a criminal mischief charge for kicking out a window of the police car with the leg that wasn't broken although it was swollen terribly by the baton of a cop who kept him from getting out through the broken window.

This time he was sent to the Ramsey One Unit, after the usual introduction and evaluation at the Diagnostic Unit. He could have done this sentence in a few years and gotten out again. Instead, he soon had over 300 years to serve.

CHAPTER SEVEN

O riginally named Texas Prison System, it was called the Texas Department of Corrections (TDC) when Rickie Smith and Keith Price came in. Now, it's the Texas Department of Criminal Justice (TDCJ). Our story began during a particularly dynamic time in the prisons. Ramifications of the considerable turmoil during the 1980s helped make Rickie what he became. Also, his personal code of honor and the determination to be respected affected the prison system. There are complete books written about the many problems and changes which tore through the prisons for more than a decade. We'll settle for a brief summary that helps to explain Rickie Smith's prison life and also had significant impact in Keith Price's life and career.

Just a few months before Rickie Smith began his first sentence, while Keith Price was a lieutenant at the Eastham Unit, a remarkable letter was sent to TDC Director W. J. Estelle from Austin MacCormick, executive director of the Osborne Association, the foremost prison watchdog and consulting body in the nation. MacCormick himself was considered the leading penologist in America. He had been assistant director of the US Bureau of Prisons, New York City Commissioner of Corrections, professor and acting dean of criminology at the University of California, and consultant on correctional problems for the US Army. Early in his career he and a colleague had surveyed every prison-type facility in the country in 1927–28. Then he helped guide reforms and reorganizations in many states, including Texas.

Here are excerpts from that letter to Director Estelle in May, 1977:

I have visited the Texas prison system many times since 1919 … it has made steady progress toward supremacy in the correctional systems of the country: first under directors (O. B.) Ellis and (Dr. George) Beto, and now under you…. I am ready to rate it as number one in the nation.

What makes that letter remarkable is that thirty-three years earlier, in 1944, MacCormick was brought in by the Texas Prison Board to make a survey. He found it to be "among the worst in the United States." His written report listed the most crucial weaknesses: inefficient administration, poorly-qualified personnel, antiquated farming methods, paucity of industries, bad living and working conditions, brutal discipline, heel-string cuttings and other self-mutilations by prisoners, an excessive escape rate, inadequate medical services, and an almost total lack of rehabilitation programs. (Heel-string cuttings were the most desperate actions taken to disable oneself from having to work in the fields.) Three years later, he sent a long telegram to then governor Beauford Jester, listing the main points of his report and stating that little had been done to change the dismal state of affairs. He said that heel-string cutting ran almost one hundred per year in Texas but such acts of desperation were almost never found in any other prisons in America.

Governor Jester began pushing for reform. Within a few months the Prison Board induced O. B. Ellis to become general manager of the Texas system. Ellis had gained a reputation of excellence as superintendent of the Shelby County Prison Farm in Memphis, Tennessee. The governor helped get the press and the public involved in pressing for major reforms in all areas of prison operation. Ellis brought a real transformation during his twelve years. After his untimely death in 1961, a former member of the Prison Board, Dr. George Beto, an educator and Lutheran minister, agreed to take the helm. He had been a strong influence in the reforms as a board member and then continued the progress as director of the Texas Department of Corrections (TDC). Not only were conditions for inmates changed dramatically, virtually eliminating heel-string cuttings and other self-mutilations, but prison industries were bringing in an average of two million dollars a year in revenue. Educational, religious, and medical services had been developed which impressed Austin MacCormick and other observers. Dr. Beto was instrumental in the establishment of the Institute of Contemporary Corrections at Sam Houston State University for training professional prison personnel, where Keith Price graduated. (Shortly after Price graduated, Beto retired from TDC to lead and teach in the Criminal Justice Program at the university.) Sam Houston State is located in Huntsville, adjacent to the Walls Unit of TDC. It was named for Sam Houston, who led the army that gained independence from Mexico and became president of the Republic of Texas. When Texas became a state he was a United States senator and then governor, but when the legislature voted to secede and join the Confederacy, Houston left office and retired in Huntsville.

Reforming one of the worst prison systems required so much more than changing operations and procedures. The public's lack of interest was reflected in the legislature and other branches of government. Prison had not been important in the early history of Texas. There were cursory attempts at a penitentiary when the territory belonged to Mexico and in the few years as a sovereign republic, but when statehood came those feeble efforts had still done very little.

The Civil War brought a bit more accomplishment, primarily because it created a market for cotton and wool which could be produced by prisoners. Following the war, Texas tried to contract out prison operations to private operators who would feed, house, and control inmates as labor for agriculture, construction, and other industries. Frequently, prisoners, in effect, became the slaves replacing those emancipated by the war. Some contractors failed miserably while a few made lots of money. Sometimes the state made money on a few contracts. But nearly always the inmates paid a high price through mistreatment and abuse. Finally the state gave up, ended all private contracts and began to operate its prisons, but inmates were not much better off. Along the way, the prevailing attitude of lawmakers seemed to have become 'prisons should make money rather than cost taxpayers.'

As already mentioned, there are many books written about various aspects of the sad and disgraceful history of prisons in Texas, and the first 100 years of that history are not germane to the Rickie Smith story. But here is a brief philosophical summary that might help explain Texas then (and now):

Texas epitomized the frontier, where life was hard. It was "every man for himself." Neighbors, and even communities, would band together to help each other, but the most recognized law was "survival of the fittest." Then, in reaction to the Reconstruction era imposed on the former Confederate States by the so-called carpetbagger governments, Texans universally accepted the theory that 'the best government is the least government.'

The new state constitution of 1876 was deliberately designed to give minimum authority to the state so it couldn't interfere with local governments and individuals. The office of governor was intended to be largely a figurehead with no real powers. The few governors of Texas who have been effective were those who could accomplish things through personal charisma and leadership. Likewise, the legislature was hampered by constitutional restrictions. Still, today, lawmakers can only meet about four months every two years and they receive only token pay—greatly restricting which citizens can afford to serve. The constitution is so restrictive that many local matters have to be submitted to a statewide vote to amend the constitution. It has been amended close to 500 times in 138 years.

In the frontier, there was a different view of crime from areas with higher density of population. When there are many acres, or even miles, between people, you learn to take care of problems yourself rather than calling a policeman. A killing could be seen as the end of an argument, but stealing a horse was a serious felony.

Prisons are usually low on anyone's priority list and, in this context, concern for penitentiaries and inmates was almost nonexistent. So it's not surprising that well into the 1900s, the state of Texas paid little attention to the needs of prisoners and the operation of prisons. After the state took charge, things improved some. Actually, the improvements brought Texas prison conditions up—to the level that Austin MacCormick called the worst in the nation in 1944 and 1947. So that helps us understand how truly remarkable it was for MacCormick to write the letter thirty years later stating that he was rating Texas prisons as the best operated in the nation.

The celebration was short-lived, however. A year after the country's foremost penologist gave it the number one rating, the State of Texas was in federal court trying to defend its prison system. The judge declared that Texas prisons were operated in violation of the US Constitution, Eighth Amendment, by using inhumane treatment of its inmates. There are a number of books that analyze prison operation, the lengthy trial, and the implementation of the court's orders. For our story of Rickie Smith, here is a quick overview.

Back in the 1800s, some prison wardens figured out that they could utilize the normal dynamics of human nature to help control the people they were responsible for. Some inmates were natural leaders and had influence over other prisoners. By giving some of those leaders incentives to exercise their influence in more structured and positive ways, there was less open violence and other problems for the prison authorities to deal with. This unofficial process grew within the system but varied greatly from one prison unit to another. Eventually, most cell blocks were under the informal control of one or more inmates called various names like "floor boys" and eventually came to be known as "building tenders." In exchange for status, recognized by prison guards and administrators, the BTs (building tenders) would see that their cell blocks were kept clean and inmates caused less trouble for the guards.

All but serious matters were handled by the BTs and their assistants. Often, the BT had access to "weapons" which were prohibited, such as pipes, clubs, sometimes even knives.

Building tenders became "elite" inmates. They were generally excused from regular work assignments—usually hard labor in the fields from sun up to sun down-they had access to prison officials and, best of all, they were able to run things within their cell block as they wished, meaning they could get favors (errands, food, sexual, etc.) from other inmates. In exchange, they would inform officials of potentially disruptive plans for fights, drugs, escapes, and so forth. Their cell doors were usually left open, giving them freedom of movement in certain areas.

Inmates were also selected to fill other jobs, such as clerks and bookkeepers, again giving them access to information about other inmates, association with guards and administrators, and better work environment than in the fields. These inmates had some influence on job and housing assignments of others.

Eventually, guidelines were developed for the selection and functioning of these co-opted inmates. Rather than being handled in-house on each prison unit, the system tried to standardize those jobs for all prisons. Naturally, even when made an "official position," treatment of inmates by building tenders varied greatly according to the personalities involved. But they improved the security and peace of the prisons within the limited funds and paid personnel the state provided.

When O. B. Ellis started the prison reforms sought by Governor Jester in 1948, one of his goals was to phase out the building tenders. But his twelve years were dominated by the tremendous challenges of improving treatment of convicts, creating programs for medical care, industry and education, changing the attitudes, pay and working conditions of officers, and upgrading severely neglected facilities. He tightened supervision of BTs but found no practical way to eliminate their contribution to prison operation before his sudden death. Ellis' successor, Dr. George Beto, likewise had a personal preference for not allowing some inmates to control others, but he too could not afford to divert the tremendous resources that would be required to provide the same amount of security and smoothness of operation with paid officers and staff. Beto did greatly improve the process of selection and supervision of BTs and instituted uniform guidelines to be followed throughout the prison system. He gained the nickname "Walking George" by personally visiting all prison units frequently—often unannounced. He showed up at night and other off-duty hours walking alone into the cell blocks, dormitories, industries, classrooms, and offices talking informally with guards and inmates alike as he went. He had a heartfelt concern for individuals and made changes based on what he learned. But the building tenders and other inmate assignments were too important to the system to be eliminated.

While it was never acknowledged openly, the building tender system was a significant ingredient in the operation of the Texas Department of Corrections which Austin MacCormick rated as the best in the nation in 1977. At that time, Beto's successor as director of TDC, W. J. Estelle, had been at the helm five years and continuing the smooth operation that Ellis and Beto had worked for.

The Texas Department of Corrections had much to be proud of. Treating and housing of inmates was improved immeasurably. Industries were productive—serving prisons and other state agencies and teaching useable skills to convicts. They made uniforms, brooms, dentures, repaired school buses, and other things. Medical care was good—better than many inmates had on the outside. Education was exemplary—a system-wide, accredited primary and secondary school district and growing access to college-level courses. Low paid "guards" recruited from nearby farms had been replaced by trained, professional "officers" and instead of nearly autonomous wardens, prisons were guided by an efficient, structured administrative system. Naturally, human nature is not perfect but problems were usually discovered and dealt with quickly. Officially, at least, inmates had avenues for complaints and recourse for significant abuses. All this required money and determined energy. Administrators were committed to the task and as they could show progress, the state legislature and political leaders rewarded their efforts with funding.

Just bringing the prisons up to standard was a gargantuan task, but it was complicated by dynamics in society at large. Texas had a growing population which automatically provided more prisoners. But during the 1960s and 1970s, social turmoil caused what could be called the 'law and order backlash.' The increasing breakdown of family structures and a growing resistance to authority supplied a larger pool of lawbreakers as candidates for prison. In 1970, Dr. Beto lamented the fact that nearly three-fourths of his prisoners were from 'broken homes.' In much of the country, citizens demanded a tougher stance against criminals. This was especially true in Texas with its heritage of frontier justice. Laws were passed mandating longer prison sentences and less "coddling" of felons with probation and early releases. Even relatively minor drug offenses could bring years in prison. The combination of more convictions and longer incarcerations brought an explosion of population in Texas prisons.

The reform of the prison system began with a population of 5,000 inmates in 1947. When the basic improvements had been made there were three times as many—over 15,000 in 1971. That makes it doubly remarkable for TDC to achieve that number one rating—handling exponential growth and completely changing the nature and operation of the system at the same time. The growth continues: the number of convicts in 1971 nearly doubled in the next ten years, to almost 30,000 in 1981. During the next twenty-five years the number of inmates increased 500 percent to 160,000 in 2006—the third largest prison operation in the country. The federal prison system and California are some larger, but Texas has almost twice the inmates of the next largest, Florida.

Apparently, while bringing Texas prisons into the modern era of the mid twentieth century and keeping up with tremendous growth, it was not a priority to change issues related to the use of force for keeping peace in prison—whether by officers or building tenders. Only the most serious incidents were addressed outside of the individual prison units. The overall record was favorable, with very few murders or escapes and significant reduction in recidivism, the rate of released inmates who return to prison. Texas—citizens and officials alike—was pleased with the good job of TDC.

As you would expect, some inmates had a different perspective. The vast majority got along with prison life, whether using the opportunity to learn from past mistakes or just learning how to keep from getting banged up. But a few were continually at war, doing battle against "the man." For a very small number, like Rickie Smith, that war was physical and a losing cause (as we'll see in subsequent chapters). For others it was a war of legal battles.

During the 1960s and 1970s, a few inmates spent their idle time researching laws and writing letters to lawyers and judges to complain of how they were being treated or how prison employees are breaking laws or prison rules. They gained the nickname "writ writers" and were largely ignored, except perhaps to be given more work and less idle time. Sometimes, a relative or friend or a lawyer on the outside would take up the cause and advance the complaints. During that time, as TDC was enjoying its reputation of success, the writ writers' petitions that actually made it to a judge or into a court were largely thrown out or settled in favor of TDC. Most judges would take the position that these are administrative matters within the system and not a real legal issue. Also, the press generally ignored routine complaints of convicts. So, the writ writers filled their idle time but accomplished little else. Dr. George Beto was very effective in advancing the reputation of TDC in official circles. He was well known and liked in Austin, the state capital city, where he had been president of Concordia Lutheran University, and he was a favorite guest for hunting, dining, and other good-ole-boy get-togethers with movers and shakers in Houston, an hour's drive from Huntsville. Since most of the writ writers' work went to local judges or to courts in Austin or Houston, they were received with some skepticism.

One writ writer, David Ruiz, was persistent. (He was persistent in criminal behavior, too. He had been arrested thirty times, in state reformatories four times as a juvenile, served eight years in TDC on a twelve-year sentence for robbery, and less than a year after his release in 1968 he was back for armed robbery.) He not only filed petitions on his own behalf, complaining of treatment and conditions, he also began helping other inmates file complaints. There were a few successes among the writ writers, including a case in which the judge determined that prisoners have the right of access to law books and legal cases. TDC had rules against inmates possessing such material in their cells, but now had to accommodate them. Eventually, in 1971, Beto moved all known writ writers to the same prison unit, apparently so they could be watched better and to keep them from helping other inmates. Dr. Beto insisted that allowing an inmate to act as a legal adviser gave him power over the other inmates. The system appointed an attorney to be a legal advisor to inmates and for a time courts accepted that as sufficient.

In 1972, after George Beto retired and W. J. Estelle became director of TDC, David Ruiz filed a handwritten petition in federal court in the Eastern District of Texas, located in Tyler. The Judge was William Wayne Justice, appointed by President Lyndon Johnson in 1968. Ruiz had filed enough writs to learn about the process and he had received help from some outside attorneys crusading for prisoner rights. The Eastern District was chosen because of Judge Justice's growing reputation as an activist, liberal judge. Only two of TDC's fifteen prisons were located in the Eastern District. One of those was the Eastham Unit and it was there that Ruiz alleged he was subjected to unconstitutional treatment. At the time of filing, Ruiz was in the Wynne Unit in Huntsville with the other writ writers. The petition listed the use of inmate building tenders, inadequate medical care, harassment for his legal work, and confinement in punitive segregation. Other inmates also filed writs in the Eastern District Federal Court raising other issues related to the operation of TDC. Judge Justice combined others with Ruiz and made it a class action suit, broadened to include all units of Texas prisons, including the thirteen not in his district. He appointed a famous prisoner rights attorney, William Bennett Turner, to represent Ruiz and ordered the US Department of Justice, including the FBI, to investigate the prisoners' complaints and participate in the proceedings.

'Ruiz vs. Estelle' became the longest prisoner's lawsuit in American history. Judge Justice issued the beginning orders in April 1974. Motions, hearings, arguments, and investigations took four years. Then the actual trial took a year, involving 161 days in court, with 349 witnesses and 1,530 exhibits. After the trial concluded, it took the judge over fourteen months to prepare his opinion that conditions in the Texas Department of Corrections constituted "cruel and unusual punishment" in violation of the Eighth Amendment of the US Constitution. In December 1980, he ordered changes in nine sections: Overcrowding, Security and Supervision, Health Care, Discipline, Access to Courts, Fire Safety, Sanitation, Work Safety and Hygiene, and Unit Size, Structure and Location. He appointed a special master to monitor compliance and report to the court which would maintain supervision of the prison system for an indefinite period.

The state appealed Judge Justice's decision. A year later, the three-judge panel of the Fifth Circuit Court of Appeals agreed that "TDC imposes cruel and unusual punishment on inmates in its custody as a result of the totality of conditions in the prisons." However, the Fifth Circuit modified or overturned some of the provisions in Justice's order saying TDC can decide how to accomplish some matters like reducing overcrowding, training officers, and where to build new prisons.

There were three issues that would be the most difficult for TDC to do.

>First is elimination of the building tender system. During the trial, officials denied the existence of building tenders but other testimony disagreed. After the trial, BTs were renamed SSIs (support service inmates). Finally, in May 1982, after the legal avenues were exhausted, the prison board agreed to dismantle the building tender system and to limit SSIs to clerical and janitorial duties—under direct supervision of staff. It took more time for that order to work through the system.

>Second is elimination of brutality. This involves severe restrictions on any use of force by officers. They had always been allowed to be physical

when it seemed necessary in dealing with an inmate problem. Being effective in the use of force often helped an officer to advance.

>And the third issue is providing adequate space for housing inmates. At the time of the trial, prisons were so full that about 5,000 convicts were the third man in a cell and sleeping on the floor. After the court order, tents were used and eventually up to 4,000 inmates lived in them. The population was growing at nearly 500 per month.

Obviously, such basic changes caused great turmoil in the prisons. It took several years to work through these requirements and find the resources to hire and train staff members and build more prisons. Judge William Wayne Justice finally ended his oversight of Texas Prisons July 1, 2002, thirty years after David Ruiz filed his handwritten petition in the federal court.

This brief summary of extremely complex events is background for the amazing story of Rickie Smith who has been an inmate in Texas prison for over thirty years. It was during those especially turbulent years in the 1980s that Rickie gained his reputation as "the most violent man in Texas prisons" and added 297 years to his initial ten-year sentence.

CHAPTER EIGHT

Rickie Smith was sitting in his cell with the door open. He was struggling with those persistent thoughts, *I'm not any good. I've made a mess of my life. I'm just a drug addict and a convict. I'll never amount to anything—like my daddy said.*

A nice young man stepped into the doorway.

"Hello, my name is Ronnie—can I talk with you?" He wore thick glasses and reminded Rickie of the cartoon TV character, Mr. Peabody.

"Well, what about?" Rickie said.

"I'd like to tell you about my friend," Ronnie replied.

"Who's your friend?" Rickie asked, looking around for someone else.

Ronnie started, "His name is Jesus...."

Before he could finish the sentence, Rickie jumped up menacingly and cussed him out. Ronnie jumped back out of the cell with a shocked look on his face. Rickie concluded his tirade with, "Don't you ever come back here, again," and added more expletives. Ronnie disappeared. He was with a religious group that came into the prison to conduct a service in the gym.

Rickie kicked the bunk, paused, took a deep breath, and stepped out of his cell. He glanced around the cell block, then walked down to the end where the tough guys were gathered and announced, "All right, if you want me, I'll join your gang."

They looked at him a few seconds then one stuck out a hand and arm covered with tattoos and said, "Welcome, Brother." Then they gathered around Rickie and began to tell what it means to be in the Aryan Brotherhood. They gave him some drugs, started tattooing their gang symbol on his arm, and explained that they live by the Aryan Brotherhood slogan, "LOVE, LOYALTY AND RESPECT."

Rickie liked those words. He had been back in the Texas Department of Corrections less than three months when he announced to his new "family" this very deliberate and fateful decision, "I may be a worthless convict, but these people are for sure gonna respect me."

When Rickie had returned to prison in the fall of 1983 at twenty-eight years of age, he was assigned to the Ramsey One Unit. Ramsey Farm had been a huge prison but was divided into Ramsey One, Two, and Three. Rickie came angry and uncooperative plus he was physically ill with no source for heroin or other drugs and still having pain from his injuries in the motorcycle wreck. A group of tough, hardened inmates who pretty much ran their own cell block where Rickie was assigned tested him, but he stood up for himself adequately and they had invited him to join them. He was not inclined to follow a crowd so he stayed away, even though he had known a few of them on the outside and met some during his first prison term. Now, suddenly, he was one of them.

As already discussed, TDC was in turmoil. The federal judge had banned the use of inmates as agents of the administration to control other inmates and TDC had finally disbanded the building tender system. But there was no way yet to hire enough officers to replace the BTs, so violence was rampant. Gangs were forming among inmates to assert protection and control. Most gangs were created within ethnic groups. The dominant gang in Rickie's area was the Aryan Brotherhood (AB). On the surface, its main purpose was to control the black inmates who would gang-rape white guys, take their commissary or whatever else they wanted. Of course the black inmate's response was to form their own gang, the Mandingo Warriors.

The Aryan Brotherhood began, like many prison gangs, in California at San Quentin. A group of white inmates called themselves Blue Bird

Gang. As black and Hispanic gangs grew in size and impact in the mid 1960s, Blue Birds made a plan. Taking the provocative name, Aryan Brotherhood, they started recruiting drives and became more active and assertive—violent. As gang members got out of prison and moved out of California, they would frequently land in other prisons and formed new chapters of their gang.

The year Rickie joined, 1983, the FBI accused the Aryan Brotherhood of aligning with mafia groups to provide physical protection for mobsters incarcerated in the Federal Bureau of Prisons. In exchange, organized crime syndicates paid money to Aryan Brotherhood and would let paroled members into their racquets on the outside. Besides protecting mafia people, AB became well enough organized to run gambling and extortion operations and to buy and sell "punks" (slang for sex slaves) inside federal prisons.

In Texas when Rickie joined, the AB seemed to have its hands full fighting other gangs and keeping up with drug needs. Brotherhood guys spent most of their time together. They would joke and play games and sports together which helped to pass the time. The normal prison routine was to leave cell doors open during the day so inmates could move around within the cell block. The AB had established pipelines for bringing in drugs and access to fruit and whatever they needed from the kitchen to make homemade wine. So life was good—for being in prison. Of course, they also were ready to respond to activities and threats from "outsiders"—especially black inmates. Weapons were plentiful, mostly crude knives, and violence was routine. Looking out for one another created the "family bond" among Brotherhood members which helped Rickie and the others to feel better. It gave them a sense of being important and needed. Rickie felt that he had what he had always sought on the outside—a group of friends who cared about him and he could trust. He was member number 17. The Aryan Brotherhood (AB) grew to twenty-three members in Ramsey One and within their cell blocks, they seemed to pretty much have control. In effect, they functioned as replacement BTs.

Guards mostly stayed out of the way, controlling access points in and out of the cell blocks, but little interference inside. System-wide, the ratio was one guard to twelve inmates and they were spread over three shifts during each 24 hours. But that was the same ratio as when there were building tenders who were pretty much on duty 24 hours per day within their cell block. Only when an inmate was hurt badly enough to require medical attention or got fed up enough to file a complaint against others did the guards get involved. The court had prescribed a ratio of 1 officer for every 4 inmates, instead of the 1 for every 12 inmates at that time, but it took years to reach that level.

Gradually, AB members were spread out to Ramsey Two and Three, and the gang bosses extended their authority to those units also. They used trustee inmates as couriers to send orders, deal drugs, and enforce rules to the other units. Trustees drove tractors and had other jobs that enabled them to move from one area to others. ('Trustees' is the title of convicts who have earned trust to be outside the normal controls without trying to escape.) The Brotherhood even extended its "business" into dealing in leather goods and other crafts inmates made, bartering for drugs and other favors.

Aryan Brotherhood members cultivated certain officers—targeted because they sympathized with white supremacy ideals or because they were financially vulnerable to payoffs. One particular inmate was very good at making leather goods. They would get guards to take them out, sell them, and buy drugs to bring back in. Seemingly innocent conversations with guards could reveal concerns over debts or family needs. Then some could be enticed to do favors in exchange for money to help with their problems. AB members not only got drugs from guards but Buck knives, straight razors, and other potential weapons. Getting an officer involved in a small infraction could be used to blackmail him to do other things. They also intimidated a key inmate who was a clerk in the major's office so he would help AB members get the prison job assignments they preferred.

Rickie used his injuries from the motorcycle wreck as an excuse to not have to work. He spent a lot of time cooking wine, rolling marijuana joints, and plotting how to work the system. When he joined the gang, he knew that drugs were flowing freely and soon he saw that blood was also flowing. Initially, the violence was focused on controlling black inmates, which appealed to Rickie because of his numerous bad experiences involving African-Americans in Atlanta and Houston. He was not as comfortable with the increasing attacks on others.

But there was real war between the Aryan Brotherhood and the Mandingo Warriors. There were killings on both sides. They grew botulism cultures and spread it around. Some guys gathered enough sulfur from matches to make a bomb and blow up a Warrior. This was in 1984 which was the worst year for violence in the Texas prison system up until then. Before the federal court intervened, there would be one to three inmate murders per year—none some years—but in 1984 there were twenty-five murders among the total of 404 reported assaults. Of course many assaults were not reported.

Rickie found himself in the middle of one example of the growing conflict in Texas prisons. Moving inmates to other units to reduce the concentration of gang members caused some interference with gang routines. Two AB honchos had pooled their money to pay for a guard to bring them a pound of marijuana. One of them, Bruce, took three ounces of weed with him when he was moved to Ramsey 3 and wanted the rest of his half pound sent over, but the partner refused. There was an angry argument between them carried on through scribbled messages carried between Ramsey 1 and Ramsey 3 by trustee inmates using farm equipment on the farms. It was called 'tractor mail.' Rickie told Bruce to give in—"Don't argue about the drugs. We can get plenty of them"—but he wouldn't give in. Finally, the AB bosses decided Bruce's ugly complaints warranted a contract to be put on his life. That violated Rickie's personal moral code of keeping your word and being fair, as well as the AB code of LOVE, LOYALTY AND RESPECT. He took the boss to task, saying, "Give me a reason for killing one of our own, maybe over some violation of our code, but certainly not over marijuana. Send a message that our principles are to be upheld, but not over stupid drugs."

So the boss responded to Rickie, "Since you want to get involved in this, then you are ordered to kill Bruce. If you don't, then a contract will be put on you."

Otherwise, prison life was pretty much the same while Rickie was on Ramsey 3, but he didn't stay long. He went on a drug binge, hopped-up on methamphetamines for three days with no sleep, when he decided he needed some fresh air and sunshine. He went outside and sat down on some welding equipment in the sun. He was there just a few minutes when a black inmate came over, "Get off my machine!"

"No way. I ain't movin'!" Rickie declared.

This was on a large concrete slab where the building made a U shape which funnels to the door where inmates go in and out to their jobs in the fields, barns, and workshops. There was a shower area next to the door where they showered after work before going into the building. The inmate walked across and into the kitchen. In a minute he came out, headed towards Rickie.

"I said that's my welder! Get off!"

Rickie assumed the inmate had gotten a knife and he saw two other black inmates over by the shower and thought they were backing the welder, so he pulled out a buck knife and stabbed him in the side.

The wounded man started running out towards the yard and the fence. With the knife in one hand, Rickie grabbed an 'aggie'—nickname for a hoe—with the other and gave chase. By then, the picket, an officer in a guard tower, sounded an alarm and had a rifle trained on Rickie. Guards came from several directions with clubs, shovels, and other 'weapons' and shielded the wounded man, telling Rickie to surrender. Instead, he wheeled around and headed back toward the building. When he was cornered there, he dropped his weapons and they swarmed him, inflicting numerous bruises and a few cuts. Officers in Texas prisons do not carry guns in the cell blocks and yard areas where inmates are. That long-standing rule is to keep inmates from getting hold of guns, but it means officers are limited to batons and their own hands for keeping order.

There were no charges from that incident, apparently attributed to gang war violence which was rampant. The next day, Rickie was moved to Eastham, the unit where he had spent the latter part of his first prison term. Violence was even worse there. Eastham was featured in a *Newsweek* cover article called "Inside America's Toughest Prison" referring to the violence of the mid 80s towards the end of and after the building tender system. There were stabbings almost daily.

There were thirteen AB members at Eastham when Rickie arrived. The gang boss' orders to kill Bruce were still active, so one day Rickie met twelve in the cafeteria, reviewed the marijuana feud, and said, "If you think I made a wrong decision on that other farm, then kill me before I leave here." He had a knife and they all had knives. "If you think I've made a right choice, then stand behind me." They all agreed he was right. That greatly aggravated the power struggle within the gang and there were AB members stabbing other members, but the feud over killing Bruce just kept simmering.

Rickie sensed that he was being intentionally put into very dangerous situations, by prison officials, where he could be hurt or killed. He was housed in a cell block with known Mandingo Warriors. Fights and skirmishes were routine. So were drugs and homemade wine. As long as it stayed within cell blocks and did not require official attention, the outnumbered and overworked guards were able to deal with it. But wars tend to grow.

The standing rule in cell block day rooms was that the inmates present would vote on what program to watch on the dayroom television set. One day when Rickie had been enjoying some homemade wine, he went into the dayroom where about forty black inmates were watching a program. He went over by the TV and declared it was time to vote on what to watch. He knew the vote would be forty to one, but he was determined they would follow the rule. They ignored him, so he pulled the plug on the set and left. The next day the guard captain came, with information from one of the Mandingo Warriors, and searched Rickie's cell. He found a knife and could tell that Rickie was drunk again, so he hauled him to his office. He gave him an appropriate lecture and declared that Rickie had to go into administrative segregation. But then he said that he understood that a man had to stand up for himself and he would let him go back to his cell.

Something changed because a short time later, Rickie was called in for a formal administrative segregation hearing with two other officers present. The infractions were discussed by the officers and the captain asked Rickie if he had anything to say in defense. Rickie responded, "If you want to send me to Ad Seg, I'll give you something to send me there for." As he spoke, even though in handcuffs, he pulled out a 12-inch shank and stabbed both the other officers in the scuffle of trying to get to the captain. They knocked him down and got out of the room, locking him in. They soon returned with other guards and S.O.R.T.—Special Operations Response Team—manned by officers specially trained to overwhelm violent offenders, hopefully without having to resort to deadly force.

They fired tear gas into the room and then swarmed Rickie. He got a fractured skull, broken ribs, numerous cuts and bruises, and both eyes swollen shut. His clothes were all torn off, shackles put on his ankles, and a chain connected from the shackles to the handcuffs. They put a baton through the chain and carried him, naked, like a butchered hog, to the infirmary. There, he lay on a bunk unable to go to the toilet or even get a drink for 12 hours. No one tended to his wounds. Then he was carried back to his cell, still hogtied.

A day or so later, he received a letter. He had to use his fingers to hold his eyes open enough to read it. It was from Marlee. (She was the girlfriend Rickie was shacked up with at the motel when Houston police arrested him for his first prison term.) Marlee was in prison again. She got probation when she and Rickie were arrested, but she had a habit of hanging around guys like Rickie who used drugs and broke laws. She worked as a topless dancer, bar maid, burglar, drug supplier, and whatever else a boyfriend might get her into.

Marlee had a tough life—beginning with being born to sixteen-year-old parents. When she was three, divorce left her with a single mom.

She always had the feeling that her mother regretted having her and when Marlee got pregnant as a young teenager, her mother forced her to have an abortion. She left home at sixteen and went to work in bars and strip clubs. She was seventeen when she took up with Rickie. Next she married a guy named Jess, who soon had her having sex with other men while he watched. She didn't like it and used more drugs, even got into heroin. This was her third prison term—drugs, stolen car, and now, drugs again. She was twenty-five years old.

She wrote Rickie that when she came to prison, this time she found Jesus. She said she cared about Rickie and knew that he needed Jesus. Rather than reacting to her caring and concern for him, he flew into a rage. Ignoring his aches and pains, he stomped and kicked around his cell and yelled curses about Marlee and Jesus for the whole cell block to hear. He was much more vehement than when Ronnie had come to invite him to a church service.

The next day, still very sore from his injuries, Rickie was moved again. This time to Ramsey 2. He was hardly settled and getting acquainted with new surroundings and people when he met a friend, Jeff Lykens. *Acquaintance* is more accurate than *friend*. They knew each other in Houston. Jeff was already in prison when Rickie came for this second term and was one of the original organizers of the Texas chapter of Aryan Brotherhood. He helped recruit Rickie into the gang, but now they are on opposite sides of the split in the gang and Jeff had gotten orders to eliminate Rickie because he had argued about the marijuana and respecting each other, and especially because a sizeable number of members took his side.

Because they were both prison-gang troublemakers, Rickie and Jeff were locked up in the Administrative Segregation cells at Ramsey 2. This means they were handcuffed before their cell door was opened and they were escorted by officers anytime they are out of their cell. Routinely, they were only taken out each day for recreation and a shower. Meals were brought to their cells. After Rickie arrived in the cell block, he and Jeff 'discussed' the differences of opinion that was splitting the gang.

Discussion in that setting means yelling up and down the row of cells, over the radios, TV, toilets flushing, talking, and other noises as well as convicts yelling at each other. It's heard by other inmates and guards alike.

Then one day, as guards escorted Rickie past other cells to the shower, Jeff slung his arm through the bars and speared a stiff heavy wire a couple of inches into Rickie's chest. It was the bale of a mop bucket that had been straightened and sharpened to a point.

There was lightning-fast reaction. The officers took off for the door out of the cell block and Rickie grabbed the spear, ripping it away from Jeff and out of his own chest. Jeff also moved fast, grabbing a kitchen ladle that had been fashioned into a large knife to renew the attack. But this time, Rickie struck first and used Jeff's own wire spear to stab him rather deeply in the side. They eyed each other through the bars. By then, the guards returned with reinforcements and the joust was over.

As usual in such inmate-on-inmate violence, the wounds received no medical attention. The staff of the beleaguered Texas prison system could only react properly to the worst incidents and inmate-on-officer violence got most of the attention. That incident did cut short Rickie's stay at Ramsey 2 and he went to one of the oldest prison units, Ellis (now called Ellis 1 since there is a newer Ellis 2). The Ellis Units are named for O. B. Ellis, who began the long journey of Texas prison reform forty years earlier.

At the Ellis Unit, Rickie and other really bad guys went to cell block J23 which was borrowed from the wing of the prison set aside as death row and designed to house inmates awaiting execution. The isolation and security was another of the many ideas prison officials tried as they sought to reduce violence in the wake of Judge William Justice's order to eliminate "unconstitutional treatment" of inmates.

Another step was to begin bringing formal charges for crimes inmates committed in prison, rather than just dealing with them in administrative processes. The Governor's Office created a Special Prosecution Unit so inmate crimes would not overburden local county prosecutors. So, a week or two after arriving at Ellis, Rickie Smith was formally charged with attempted murder of one of the officers he had stabbed in the captain's office at Eastham. That required him to be officially arraigned on the charges in court by a state district judge. The other guard's wound was less serious and not called attempted murder.

Meanwhile, at Eastham, an event took place that would play a part in Rickie's life. A Mandingo Warrior named Earnest Ross killed an Aryan Brotherhood member named Jones. Rickie didn't know either of them, but was told about it and that the AB 'steering committee' said Ross must die.

December 6, 1984: Rickie Smith and some other inmates were escorted onto a prison bus and taken to the Diagnostic Unit at Huntsville, where they were transferred into the custody of the sheriff of Houston County to be transported to the courthouse in Crocket because their alleged crimes occurred at Eastham, in Houston County. They were combined with inmates from Eastham also being taken to that court. There, the inmates took turns standing before the judge, listening to the charges filed against them and entering a plea. The natural response was, "Not guilty." After Rickie's turn he was sitting in the courtroom, looking for a chance to use the large 'shank' he had in his underwear on either David Wheat or Royce Smithey, special prosecutor and special investigator from the Governor's Office. He had met them as they investigated the incident that brought the charge of attempted murder. He never got a chance to stab Wheat or Smithey in that courtroom, but he recognized the name when Earnest Ross was called before the judge to enter a plea to the charge of murdering AB member Jones.

When they left the courthouse, Rickie's attention turned to Ross. The bus brought the inmates back to the Diagnostic Unit to be processed back into the custody of the Texas Department of Corrections. That involved going into a large holding room, where all inmates entered prison. They stood in a single file line, removed all clothing except underpants. Then each one, in turn, removed the underpants for inspection before being allowed to redress and get on the bus to go back to their prison unit.

Rickie, knowing he could no longer conceal the shank, decided to use it. Suddenly, he burst through a clump of guards, pushed the deputy sheriff out of the way, and sank the homemade knife into Ross's chest. Immediately the deputy recovered, grabbed a chain, and started beating Rickie until he almost lost consciousness. Ross was hurried to the hospital and Rickie went to isolation. The knife did not go through vital organs or arteries, but it was bad enough to bring a second charge of attempted murder against Rickie.

A S.O.R.T. team took Rickie back to Block J23 at Ellis 1. The warden at the Diagnostic Unit notified the rest of the Texas Department of Corrections that Rickie Smith was banned from coming to that unit, even to just change transportation vehicles. Anytime he was to be moved, it would have to be by special transportation van handled by S.O.R.T.

Three weeks later, Christmas Day 1984, Rickie turned thirty. Then, when you are thinking it couldn't get any worse, on New Year's Day it did.

There was a TV set mounted on the wall across the hall from the row of cells and for New Year's Eve, the TV was left on past normal lights out time so inmates could watch a Willie Nelson Special bringing in 1985. When Willie Nelson went off, so did the TV. Rickie couldn't sleep as usual, so he got a Louis L'Amour western novel and lay down on the bunk with his head by the bars so he could read by the light coming from the hallway.

Around 2:00 in the morning, a shadow passed across the pages of the book. Rickie jumped to his feet just as a spear came between the bars and hit the bunk where he had been. In an automatic, lightning-fast response, he kicked, breaking the broom handle of the spear. He tried to grab it as it went back out of the bars, then he heard the steps of the man running up the stairs of the cell block. He was certain it was a certain gang member under orders from Aryan Brotherhood leaders. He got a knife from its hiding place in the cell and waited. Apparently, the inmate had finagled a way to be out of his locked cell and into the high security cell block.

It was only a few minutes before a shadowy figure crept along the bars of cells until he reached Rickie's. He then quickly moved out of reach in front of Rickie and, in one motion, lit a cigarette lighter, touched a fuse in a metal Prince Albert Tobacco can, and pitched it. Rickie reacted as soon as he saw the can, before any fire, grabbing his blanket and holding it up in front of himself. The burning fluid showered into the cell, catching the blanket, bedding on the bunk, books, and anything flammable on fire. The 8 foot by 12 foot cell became an instant inferno. Rickie's quick reaction with the blanket helped protect him somewhat, but he still received serious burns on his arms, face, and a few spots on his body, before guards arrived with fire extinguishers. Of course the bomber vanished as the flames began to appear.

Rickie was taken to the infirmary and the burns were treated. Very soon, the warden had been rousted from bed and came to the infirmary.

"Ok, son, I need to know who did this to you."

"I am not going to tell you, Warden," Rickie replied.

"He was trying to kill you and nearly succeeded. I want to get him and take care of this. Just tell me who it was."

Rickie shook his head and said, "It's your job to find out, Warden, and I'm not going to tell you. But take me back to J23 and very soon you'll know who it was."

"No sir! You're going to stay right here in this infirmary, where I can keep you safe. Besides, you have serious burns that have to be treated. Once more, Smith, tell me who did it."

"I will not tell you, but take me back and I'll show you so you won't have to take care of it," Rickie said with a very determined look on his face. The warden left.

The next day, a sergeant officer came into the infirmary and stopped by the window to Rickie's room. After brief chitchat, he asked who had thrown the Molotov cocktail into the cell. Rickie stood up and slugged the sergeant through the window. He left and in a very few minutes a S.O.R.T. came in and roughed up Rickie. They were not as hard as they usually were, apparently because of his burns.

Rickie was still determined to get back to J23 and take care of his attacker. That night, he realized the infirmary had a false ceiling. He made a place so he could climb into the attic. He took a couple of mattresses off the infirmary beds into the attic and set them on fire. Soon the fire spread down into the infirmary and up to the roof of the main building of the Ellis Unit. Of course, fire alarms were sounded and fire trucks came from several communities in the area and got the fire out. It was contained in the infirmary area and the building roof above it.

Guards came and gave Rickie what he wanted—they took him to his blackened sooty cell in J23. Jeff Lykens was also in a J23 cell. After an appropriate amount of name-calling, cursing, and denying things between them, Rickie convinced Jeff that he was being manipulated and used. Eventually, Jeff agreed that gang leaders had strayed far from their motto of LOVE, LOYALTY AND RESPECT. The two actually became friends that day.

Meanwhile, Rickie's other war—with the prison system—heated up—fueled by his setting fire to the building and refusing to name who set fire to his cell. In fact, the warden wrote a report on the incident which claimed that the inmate was guilty of self-mutilation in setting his own cell on fire. Also, TDC had determined that even the extra high security of death row was not adequate for Rickie Smith and a few others. They were rebuilding eighteen cells creating Super Segregation, nicknamed "Superseg." Twelve of these cells were in an isolated cell block of the Coffield Unit, near Palestine Texas, and six were in the Eastham Unit. Rickie and seventeen others will officially be recognized as the worst men in Texas prisons.

CHAPTER NINE

Rickie Smith's wars were fought during extremely turbulent times for the Texas prison system. One war was between his gang, Aryan Brotherhood (AB), and competing gangs—especially the Mandingo Warriors, the dominant black inmate gang. Another war was within the AB as factions battled over leadership and personal conflicts. But the most active battles involved Rickie trying to accomplish his stated declaration regarding the guards and the system—"These people are, for sure, gonna respect me!"

Of course, the "respect" Rickie was seeking was to be left alone to do what he wanted (drugs, booze, etc.) and recognition that he was tough enough to take whatever was done to him and to give back more. Never mind that this was prison where inmates had few rights and were expected to obey rules, respect authority, and follow instructions.

At this time, however, rules, instructions, and even authority were not that simple. Actually, what was expected of inmates was fully stated and pretty clear to everyone and the majority of inmates lived within the guidelines. What was not clear was who was really in charge in the cell blocks and how penalties were applied and transgressions dealt with. For decades, day-to-day life was governed more by "building tenders" (BTs) than by officers. Too many of these select "inmate guards" applied rules unfairly or selfishly and used varying degrees of force and violence to enforce them or to punish violators. The accepted practice, even for real prison officers, to deal with infractions was primarily physical force—especially with serious troublemakers like Rickie. Now, use of force was officially quite restricted.

Even when the appeals court agreed with Judge Justice' ruling that Texas prisons must change, it took two more years for the state to officially admit that such activity existed and it took more years to actually accomplish change. So, through much of the 1980s, there was ambiguity, confusion, and serious disagreements over how to run the prisons, particularly how to deal with problem inmates.

Many experienced officers left rather than change, which meant many new officers had to be found—a problem compounded by the court order to more than double the number of guards in relation to inmate population. Meanwhile, the number of inmates was multiplying (had doubled in ten years) so hiring new guards needed to keep up with that growth rate, too. Prison employees became divided between those favoring the old ways and those trying to follow the new guidelines. All of that made "turbulence" an understatement.

That brings us back to Keith Price.

He had been a rising star in Texas Department of Corrections. His focus in college had been to become a parole officer, but the summer he worked in the prison made him realize that was what he liked and that he had an aptitude for dealing with inmates. He made lieutenant in a year, then captain and three years later, major. Simultaneously, he got a master's degree in criminal justice and a PhD in behavioral science.

Of course, the chaos in TDC included Price—on the opposite side of Rickie's war. The young officer had some inner turmoil, too, although it stayed in the background until later. His training and his work experience was in the traditional ways of penology—as practiced in Texas—which provided recognition as one of the best prison systems in the country. However, that did not always fit with his education in behavioral science.

His conflicting instincts were featured in that major cover story (eleven pages long) in *Newsweek Magazine* in October 1986 which detailed the "perfect storm" disaster in Texas prisons, focusing on the Eastham Unit, which *Newsweek* called "America's Toughest Prison."

TDC was trying to comply with some of Judge Justice's orders while denying other problems existed. So, to reduce overcrowding—that is, three inmates in small two bunk cells—thousands were moved into tents in prison yards. *Newsweek* described how Price, a captain, was the ranking officer on duty at Eastham one night in November 1981 when 250 inmates in a tent camp went on a rampage sparked by two building tenders hassling six Hispanic prisoners. The BTs retreated to the building while the tent dwellers began setting tents on fire and made barricades of burning mattresses and other materials. (There were tents burned in other units also.)

Captain Price gathered sixty officers for a riot squad but then saw about 300 BTs and their helpers in the gym, armed with pipes and other clubs, about to charge the rioters. The warden had called out the inmate bosses, supplied pipes, and cut them into 3-foot lengths. The inmates tied white rags around their heads so they could be distinguished from the rioting convicts. Price argued with the warden that only officers should be involved, with reinforcements from other prison units. The warden refused so Price led his "troops" into the smoke-filled yard. Apparently most officers stayed inside. Soon the rioters, obviously no match for the pipes and other weapons, fled from the fires they had set, pursued by the BT squad. They could only run as far as the fence. The BTs formed what they called a 'whupping line' and chased the inmates through it into the building. There was blood everywhere and numerous inmates unconscious but, miraculously, no one was killed.

As Price surveyed the disaster and directed the recovery and restoration from the horror, he was confronted with the realization that he and other prison staff do not have real control of the prisons. He felt in his gut that he didn't want to be there anymore. Later, when the riot and response was brought up in court, the "old guard" prison officials tried to shift the blame for the assault onto Price. But actually, in the midst of the chaos, he wanted to restore order and followed the orders he had opposed to take the only action that seemed available.

The Eastham mayhem occurred two years after Federal Judge Justice issued his order to stop the use of inmate "guards" and a year after the

Federal Appeals Court upheld that decree. Six months after that night, the Texas Department of Corrections admitted the use of BTs and signed an agreement to dismantle the Building Tender System. Even then it still took time to be in compliance.

Keith Price did not follow his gut and leave and about the time TDC formally acknowledged the BTs and agreed to eliminate them, Price was promoted to major. Just two months later he was asked by court representatives and he, somewhat reluctantly, agreed to accept a newly created position in Operational Audits, designed to determine how prison staff was complying with new operational policies. Eventually, that became a pivotal role in administrative efforts to reform the Texas prison system. It involved looking into a lot of issues involving use of force in dealing with prisoners.

Soon Operational Audits was changed to Internal Affairs with Price as the supervisor.

Internal Affairs had to investigate all incidents of violence and make a report. Many of the prison units were experiencing chaos. The gangs were taking over areas of prisons and fighting each other. Drugs were rampant. There were not enough officers to take the place of building tenders, turn keys, and other inmate assistance in controlling cell blocks. Also, there were officers and other staff, including wardens, who opposed the new rules for disciplining inmates and did it the old ways, and Keith Price had gone from being one of them to becoming the enemy. He again felt that he didn't want to be there.

Along with the extremely difficult working conditions, his personal life had become what he calls "a wreck." Several years of intense job stress was breaking up his family. His wife left and took their young son. He developed a bleeding ulcer and suffered from depression. He had drifted away from church, which had been such an important part of his life growing up, so he started going to a church where he found some peace in the midst of the personal turmoil. He felt a spiritual renewal and believed that God gave him another chance which helped him. He also began a relationship with a woman who was understanding and helpful. Eventually, they married and "life started over."

While he had soured on his prison career working through personnel matters, he was promoted to warden. That gave him a new focus and got him away from the firing line of Internal Affairs. He accepted the promotion and went to the Retrieve Unit, a fairly small prison south of Houston.

That first assignment as warden was a tough job. Retrieve Unit housed about a thousand inmates, most considered "incorrigible" repeat offenders. It was torn by gang wars. It had one cell block of "lock-up" cells. Price added another lock-up cell block. Things were much better in less than two years, so Price was moved to the Darrington Unit—also full of bad guys and twice as many as in Retrieve.

Many considered Darrington a mess. Price was the sixth warden in six years. Again, he turned things around, getting control of the prison. He segregated the worst troublemakers and instituted methods of finding weapons and contraband in possession of inmates all within the new policies of the post-court order prison system. The most difficult inmates went to what became known widely as "B Line," home of the 'worst of the worst.' There they yelled and cussed all they wanted to but they were isolated from each other and from the rest of the inmates. They were fed in their cells and shields were installed to protect the officers who worked there.

Price was warden at Darrington for eight years. He was liked by the staff and respected by most of the inmates, tough but fair. He and the chaplains instituted some innovative ways of increasing contact and visitation for families of inmates which further improved the atmosphere of prison life. His personal life was much better and he and his family were involved in church and community.

We'll come back to Warden Price and the Darrington Unit later.

While things got better for Price, Rickie Smith went from bad to worse. We detailed his knife attack on two officers and trying to kill inmate Ross, plus two attempts on his life by others, and how he set fire to the building at the Ellis Unit. That was all in about six months' time. Now, he begins a new chapter.

CHAPTER TEN

SUPER-SEG! That's Rickie Smith's new home. SuperSeg was created by Raymond K. Procunier who was director of the Texas Department of Corrections only five months (instead of two years he said when hired). He said, "I have run out of gas," because of the increasing violence throughout the system. Procunier ordered the special cell blocks of Separate Segregation Units, nicknamed 'SuperSeg,' to house what he called "the cream of the crud."

Before the eighteen cells were prepared and guards trained, he was replaced in mid 1985 by Colonel O. Lane McCotter. The prison board had searched specifically for someone who could deal with the violence. McCotter was a retired army colonel and had been commander of the military prison at Fort Leavenworth in Kansas. He actually was hired as Procunier's assistant with the expectation he would move up when Procunier left. McCotter was found and recommended by Dr. George Beto, prison director from 1962 to 1972, then became professor of Corrections at Sam Houston State University. Beto was a consultant for many prison systems and recognized as a leading penologist in the nation.

After three months on the job, in September 1985, McCotter ordered a radical lockdown, confining about half of the 38,000 inmates in the twenty-six state prisons to their cells while officers tried to find weapons and other contraband. Then they began to move and separate members of gangs and to disrupt the recruiting of new gang members. Members of most gangs could be identified by the symbols tattooed on their arms and elsewhere by inmate tattoo artists. The lockdown came after seven inmate murders in a week at two prison units. In the two years since the end of the building tender system of control, known gang membership had increased tenfold. Officials had counted about 800 members of gangs. The most violent were the Mexican Mafia and the Texas Syndicate, rival Mexican and American gangs. Then came Aryan Brotherhood and Mandingo Warriors, the white and black enemies. Thousands of inmates remained confined to their cells for weeks.

Concurrent with the lockdown, on September 6, 1985, Rickie and seventeen others were moved to SuperSeg. These were the worst offenders, primarily violent gang leaders. Rickie was put in cell number 12 at the Coffield Unit.

SuperSeg cells had doors of bars overlaid with steel mesh and a "bean slot" which was locked and generally only opened for food trays and other necessities to be passed into the cell. Besides the special cell doors, prisoners were locked in 23 hours and only taken out once a day for exercise and a shower. They were required to strip as officers watched, then put on undershorts and back up to the bean slot which was unlocked for an officer to reach through and put on handcuffs. Then the door was opened and shackles were secured around the ankles. The chain between the ankle cuffs was only long enough to allow him to shuffle his feet, not to take regular steps. Two officers must accompany the inmate while he was out of the cell. Exercise was in a small "cage" and with no other inmates there. The shower was in an open stall with guards watching. Then he was cuffed behind his back and shuffled back to the cell. Little personal property was allowed in the cell. The only human interaction was with the officers and yelling back and forth with the other SuperSeg inmates. Many of the convicts in that cell block were enemies of each other in the gang wars.

Rickie was handled even more carefully than most of the other SuperSeg residents. For six months he slept on bare concrete slab, until one of the court-appointed monitors forced the warden to bring him a mattress and sheets. Also, he was kept in handcuffs when taken to the small exercise cage and the shower.

So Rickie was isolated in this cell, full of anger and hatred. He felt desperate—he had tried to stand up for himself as Red, his dad, taught him, but while he had caused much hurt, damage, and expense, he didn't seem to have gained any respect or benefit. He was in the worst part of the last place he ever wanted to be in—prison. In fact, it appeared he was a complete failure. He was in prison just like his dad and others warned him. Now he had time to think, since there was nothing else to do. But rather than think about how he could be different and try to work his way back to a more respectable life, he only thought of how he could fight back at enemies and the system. Such thoughts were encouraged by all the ugliness and anger he heard so loudly from everyone else in the SuperSeg cell block, including some officers. At this point he was focused more on the prison system than gang business.

Another innovation McCotter instituted was creation of Special Operations Response Teams (SORT) to handle the most violent inmates. Members were recruited, screened, and trained to make the prisons safer. McCotter had seen similar squads in action at the Leavenworth Military Prison. "By the time they call us, everything else has failed," one SORT member said. "We'll do the job and do it right." They were authorized to use as much force as necessary but also trained to keep their cool in tough confrontations. Of course, inmates see SORT as a 'legalized goon squad' specializing in roughing up convicts and destroying their personal belongings.

For a while, after moving to SuperSeg, there was no mail, no visits, and no personal property allowed. Feeding his anger was what felt like constant mistreatment—SORT squads would come to "shake down" the cells. Inmates had to be handcuffed behind their backs and whenever an inmate balked, the officers would twist the handcuffs, causing pain, then put the inmate naked or only in boxer shorts on the cold concrete floor, face down—sometimes "slammed" down, frequently with a steel-toed boot on the back of the neck. This treatment was apparently designed to "break" these tough guys and convince them that the officers were in control. Eventually it worked with some of the men, who became more compliant and quiet, but not Rickie. It had the opposite effect on him and he told them so, "I'm not going to put up with this. You'll have to kill me—or I'll kill you." Shakedowns were routine, weekly, with special ones added from time to time.

The regulations state that a prisoner can only be kept in segregation for thirty days at a time. Then his situation was to be reviewed to determine whether he should be taken out of segregation or kept there another month. So periodically the warden, Jack Garner at this time, would come to SuperSeg for a review. He would walk up and down the cell block, dressed up in his Western-style suit, cowboy hat and fancy ostrich-skin boots, and asked various convicts how they were and how they felt. He often used the inmate's supposedly secret gang nickname. Apparently, that was sufficient for the "review" to determine that they stayed where they were for another month. There were no formal on-the-record hearings.

By day fifty-three in SuperSeg (yes, he had been counting), Rickie decided he had to do something. He, like many others, had stockpiled feces and urine and when Warden Garner came doing his walk through, he made his move. When the warden came in range, Rickie threw his "stuff" on him—a direct hit. It not only covered his nice clothes but even went into his mouth, causing him to vomit.

That brought immediate action. A SORT squad came and roughed up Rickie, then moved him from Coffield to the Eastham Separate Segregation Unit cell block. He was placed in a cell next to a mortal enemy from a rival gang. Warden Garner had said, "I'm sending you where they will deal with you." He and the new neighbor had tried to kill each other at the Ramsey Farm.

The routine went on just like at Coffield, with Rickie giving officers a hard time and a SORT squad coming to "shake down" his cell two or three times a week—and in the process slammed him on the concrete floor, usually adding a few kicks and whacks with a baton. While Rickie was the most persistent, he was not the only inmate who gave the officers a bad time in the SuperSeg cell blocks. Eventually, they added large plastic shields on wheels. These would be rolled along between officers and the cells when guards would take food to the inmates and when taking them out for exercise and showers.

In February 1986, Rickie convinced a black inmate in the cell next door to cooperate with him in an extraordinary plan. The convincing was a combination of threat and promise of protection. Rickie had been asking for a meeting with the warden for weeks. He wanted to complain, face-to-face, about the treatment he was getting from officers. More than complain, he wanted to negotiate a truce—you treat me right and I'll not attack the guards. His requests to meet were ignored. In fact, he learned that Becky had come to visit but was told he could not have any visits. Also, he had bought a few personal items from the commissary and a SORT team tore them up, so he decided to get some attention. (His mother kept money in his inmate trust fund account for him to use in the commissary.) One evening he was able to break loose the steel plate of the bean slot in his cell. While other inmates made a lot of noise, he used the steel plate to beat a hole in the concrete wall between his cell and the neighbor's large enough for him to crawl through. They used blankets to cover the hole. Then the accomplice pretended to be ill, like having a heart attack. Rickie alerted the officers on duty that the man needed attention. They checked and took him to the infirmary, leaving his cell door open. Rickie then crawled through the hole and got out into the hallway of the cell block. He grabbed a guard, took his keys and baton, but then let him leave. He used the keys to open the doors of the other inmates' cells in SuperSeg. In the 45 minutes it took to gather an army of officers and come back to the cell block, he and the other four inmates had trashed the cell block, breaking windows, setting the plastic shield on fire, and breaking everything they could. Then Rickie made a pot of coffee, got a knife he had made, and sat down with a cup of coffee to wait. When the officers came, Rickie said he just wanted to talk with the warden about the way he was being treated and get some changes made. No inmates had escaped the cell block.

The warden was there so Rickie said, "I can't do my time here at Eastham. I've already stabbed officers and tried to stab a captain here. If I stay here, I'll end up dead or I'll end up killing somebody."

The warden listened and Rickie continued, "Before I let your officers put me in a bad position to get killed or I allow y'all to kill me, I'll kill some of them. If they put their hands on me, slam me while I'm hand-cuffed, or hurt me in any way, I will kill somebody."

The warden gave his assurance that none of that will happen. He added, "You'll be all right and I will try to get you moved to another unit." With the middle of the night meeting over, Rickie was taken to a segregation cell in another cell block since the wall he broke through had to be rebuilt.

Next day, the captain on duty brought a SORT and Rickie was soundly beaten. Bloody all over, he was carried hog-tied to the major's office and put on top of the desk. The major had to get an official report together, including the charge of "Taking Hostages" against Rickie. The major walked over, put his finger in Rickie's face, and said, "Just so we're clear regarding the conversation you had with the warden early this morning, you will NOT run this prison. I will personally see to it that you know that I decide how things are done around here—not you."

Rickie spit blood in the major's face and was immediately swarmed, slammed to the floor along with considerable stomping before the SORT took him back to the management cell.

Next day, a SORT came to shake down Rickie's cell, pushing him down to the concrete floor with his hands cuffed behind so he couldn't catch himself, and other rough treatment, just like so many times before. When they left, Rickie sat on the bare bunk and began contemplating the possible ways he could fight back—particularly planning how he could kill the captain.

A few days later, guards came and took Rickie to recreation and a shower. When he went into the shower naked, guards controlled the water and he was scalded in all hot water. The guards all laughed. Next day when they took him out, they slammed him on the concrete. An officer brought his little bit of personal property to the cell. He could see that his little radio his mother bought was in pieces. He yelled and struggled but the officers held him down. Standing by just watching was a young guard named Kervin Crooms.

Soon Rickie was moved to a special cell in that cell block that had a double door. When they took him out for exercise and shower he struggled and fought, so he was again hogtied and carried to exercise. Going through a door his head was run into the door facing hard enough to make a gash which bled so much that they took him to the infirmary. A captain came in to see about him and Rickie charged him. The captain got him down on the floor, slugging him. Rickie got up and went back after the captain, but other officers came and subdued him and put him in chains. The captain warned Rickie that he just "might lose his life." Then they took him back to his cell.

He lay down on the bare bunk to rest and try to relax from all the fight and tension of recent days. He really only rested a little before his mind began replaying the constant turmoil and battles with prison guards. He mostly ignored the yelling and cussing coming from the other cells in the wing.

I am not going to take it anymore, he thought. *It's me or them. If I make 'em kill me, it'll be over. If I kill them, I'll go to death row and I'll be better off than I am here.* He realized how extreme the thoughts he just had were, so he went back over them. Then, *I have fought them and stabbed several to the point where they are not going to leave me alone. They will continue to tear up stuff and slam me and hurt me and I will fight back and struggle. It's a vicious cycle.*

Again he reviewed his thoughts and confirmed the reality of his situation. *I can't let it go on*, he concluded, *I've got to stop it.* There was a metal bunk in this cell. He began kicking, pulling and beating it against the wall until it was torn up enough to get a strip of steel about a foot long and 2 inches wide. He spent the next couple of days "filing" the metal on the concrete floor to make a sharp point on one end. The next day as a trusty inmate was mopping the cell block hallway, Rickie waited for him to get in front of his cell then grabbed the mop. He intimidated the trusty and convinced him that he would get hurt real bad if he told that Rickie had the mop.

He got some twine from a neighbor convict called "Hollywood" and secured the sharp steel knife to one end of the wooden handle. That made a spear 4 or 5 feet long. Then he began planning how to get the captain involved in the recent beatings to come to the cell so he could kill him. He kept the spear hidden for five or six days. Surprisingly, he had been in the cell for more than a week without a shakedown or other attention from a SORT. But he had not been successful in getting the captain to come to the cell block. He knew it's only a matter of time until the spear is discovered so he thought, *I guess I better use it on someone else.* Of course, that means he had to decide who and how.

Just like previous times when he was on the verge of doing something bad to someone, there was a faint feeling of hesitation in the back of his mind. When there was a challenge or confrontation or in a dispute, he just reacted and did what seemed needed. But it's somewhat different when he was preparing to attack an unsuspecting officer. *Well, am I going to go on with this?* he said to himself. Then over and over, *Am I going to do it? Am I really going to do this?*

Later that day, Officer Kervin Crooms came to give inmates iced tea to go with supper. Rickie's thoughts solidified, *I'm going to use the spear.* His mind and body shifted into action mode as Crooms approached his cell and stepped up to the bars with the pitcher of tea.

The spear went between bars and into Crooms' abdomen. It went with such force that it sliced all the way through, almost coming out his back. It pushed him backwards across the hallway to the wall across from the row of cells, the spear handle sticking out of his abdomen.

Quickly, guards called for help. Some tried to help Crooms while others made sure the inmates were locked in their cells. Some of the inmates had immediately cheered when they saw what happened to the officer;

others looked on in stunned silence. This brazen attack was beyond what any of them had tried or even planned.

Rickie just stood at his cell door and watched. There was a sense of accomplishment that he actually won a round against the system. But deeper inside, he felt some nagging regret that he may have killed a man who had not done anything to him—other than wear the gray uniform of the enemy. Those frantically trying to get Crooms out of the cell block felt he was beyond help, but they were not about to give up trying.

As soon as the victim was moved out, swarms of officers came after Rickie with a vengeance. He was hardly out of the cell when slammed to the concrete floor then chained, hand and foot. They carried him from the cell block and out to a shower at the back door of the building and threw him on the concrete floor, exclaiming over and over and with a variety of curse words what a sorry, low down, 'blankety blank' he was.

The warden had checked on Crooms and then came just before the cluster of officers hustled Rickie out. The warden stood over Rickie and said, "My officer is dead, you b------. You're going to death row and I will personally be there to watch when you get the needle stuck in your arm." They carried him out to a prison van, slammed the door, and started out from Eastham.

During that rough ride, his thoughts went back several years. Warden Bonner was a captain at a different prison unit then, and he put a knife to Rickie's throat. It was before court orders to change the way convicts were handled. Rickie and a black inmate were being punished for repeated infractions. They worked in the fields during the day and then had to shell 2 gallons of peanuts before they could go in to bed for a while before heading back to the field in the morning.

Rickie got a friend to slip him socks full of shelled nuts. The young inmate asked him to share with him or he would tell on Rickie. Rickie warned that he would "get him" if he told, but he did anyway. Captain Bonner came and took a gallon of Rickie's shelled nuts. Rickie got up off the concrete floor they sat on to go get more unshelled peanuts, but then kicked the inmate in the face with steel-toed boots, knocking out some teeth. Then he kicked a bucket of nuts down the hall towards Captain Bonner and said, "Get your momma to shell my peanuts."

Several guards came running, tackled Rickie, then they chained his feet to his waist behind his back and cuffed his hands in the back. They used a night stick as a pole through the chains and carried him hog-tied to the floor of the captain's office. The captain put a knife to his throat and asked him what would keep him "from cutting your punk-ass throat?" In chains and cuffs Rickie knew he couldn't prevent it, so he replied, "Cut it. I can't stop you anyway." But something stopped him. (Now a warden and without the knife) Bonner again threatened Rickie's life.

After an hour of bouncing around in the van, Rickie realized they were arriving at Coffield where he had thrown feces on Warden Garner and been moved to Eastham. He was pushed and dragged to the Separate Segregation cell block and placed in cell number 12. The cell was completely bare, not even a mattress. Rickie had nothing of his own. The only clothes were undershorts. He stayed that way a long time. Eventually, an inmate several cells down the run passed a blanket from cell to cell for Rickie to use.

After a week or so, as most of the black and blue places on his body waned, his anger grew. Soon, it could only be described as rage. Besides his own hatred of the prison system in general and a number of people in particular, he was constantly bombarded with the ranting and cussing of the eleven other inmates in SuperSeg, the "cream of the crud."

By now, officers had learned more how to handle the SuperSeg inmates and manage the cell block better. They were always on alert for flying missiles and occasional tantrums with food trays and learn to tune out the constant taunts and ugly yelling. And no major incidents were recorded for a couple of weeks. But Rickie had determined that he owed the system another attack and he would kill a guard as payback for how they had treated him after the spearing of Crooms. He had not yet been notified of official charges in the Crooms case.

I've got to do something, Rickie said to himself. He and another Aryan Brotherhood member had been planning to file legal action against the system for the way they were being treated—little or no personal property, few or no visits being allowed, mail being "lost" or destroyed, being roughed up regularly by SORT, and so on. Of course these conversations were loud enough for the guards as well as inmates to hear. But Rickie had committed himself to kill another officer and he couldn't drop it—he was not going to go back on his word even if it was just to himself.

One day a SORT came in and did a routine shakedown of all twelve inmates and their cells in SuperSeg. They did the usual painful twisting of handcuffs and threw each man to the floor while ransacking his cell. They were especially rough with Rickie. That was the last straw—again. He decided he had been calm long enough. He had been checking out all possibilities and his experience in the construction business alerted him to the fact that the ceiling had been lowered which meant the air duct had to be lengthened to reach the vent in his cell. So he removed the vent cover and ripped lose one of the rods which held the duct. He sharpened it on the concrete floor into a knife about 28 inches long. The dull end was bent and wrapped in cloth. He stashed it to wait for the next time a SORT squad came.

A couple of days later, an officer had his fill of listening to Rickie and the other AB member complaining about their treatment and agreeing to file legal grievances and do other things to change the situation, and he was tired of their constant bad-mouthing the prison system and the guards. So Officer Roger White stepped in front of Rickie's cell.

"You don't deserve to even live, let alone have any rights," he said. "You have caused people to lose their life by your fighting the system and through your gangs. You don't deserve to breathe good clean air."

This was two weeks after Rickie had speared Officer Crooms.

Rickie listened to the officer venting about having to hear all their ugly, hateful complaining and especially how he had his fill of Rickie Smith.

Calmly, Rickie responded, "Well, then, bring me some toilet paper."

SuperSeg inmates were given a few sheets of toilet tissue at a time, rather than a whole roll which could be used for fires or stopping up plumbing or other creative mischief. As White left to get toilet paper, Rickie retrieved the sharp metal rod from its hiding place, thinking, *He doesn't think I deserve to live, huh? Well, I don't think he deserves to live.*

As Officer White prepared to open the bean slot to pass toilet tissue in, Rickie aimed the sharp point through the small space in the wire mesh pattern covering the door and speared the guard. White saw the rod coming out and grabbed at it, trying to stop it and pull it away from Rickie. Another officer was there and grabbed the rod, too. They got it out of Rickie's hands and began checking White. It was a bloody sight even though White had not felt the stab in the scuffle. Of course he was hurried to the infirmary for medical attention and then to the Intensive Care Unit at Anderson County Memorial Hospital in Palestine.

SuperSeg was locked down until a SORT came to remove Rickie. After manhandling him roughly, he was moved to another area. But soon he was back in the SuperSeg cell, since there was no more secure place in the prisons. The officer's wound was about 6 inches deep, in the upper abdomen area, but amazingly no vital organs were hit. The next day he insisted on checking out of the hospital over the protest of doctors.

Soon Warden Garner was in Judge Justice' Court asking that law books be banned from cells because Rickie stood on a stack of law books to reach the ceiling and get the duct brace. Judge Justice threatened Warden Garner with contempt of court for making such a request.

These were the major acts of violence by inmate Rickie Smith in the first nine months of life in both Separate Segregation Units at Coffield and Eastham Prisons even though SuperSeg was designed to prevent such things. There were many other scuffles and confrontations too, such as an effort to stab a guard in the eye with a nail, but he dodged and got stuck in the neck instead. That was shortly after the White stabbing. He certainly had earned the label "Most Dangerous Inmate" of the 40,000 in the Texas Department of Corrections.

Soon after those stabbings, a captain named Slider came to Rickie's cell and made a speech he apparently had thought about carefully, and unlike many accusations by officers, Rickie listened and this one played over and over in his head, "You are really bad! There is nothing I can do to you. The warden won't even let me write a disciplinary case. But one day you are going to kill an officer and the State of Texas is going to kill you. But that's not the bad part. Because then, you are going to stand before your Creator and give an account of your life."

"Yeah, I'm going to hell—and I'll be waiting for you there and I'll stick you with a hot poker." He added more obscenities.

Slider just stood there until he finished, then said, "You'll give an account for every word and every deed. You have gotten away with a lot in prison, but you won't get away before your, and my, Creator." He walked away.

CHAPTER ELEVEN

W e have been focusing on how Rickie Smith caused more trouble than most other inmates. There were certainly lots of other
important activities in the Texas Department of Corrections.

In spite of hard work by Keith Price and others in Internal Affairs,
the special master appointed by Judge Justice to monitor compliance on
"use of force" reported that while some progress has been made, TDC
was still not in compliance. That was shortly after Price had moved from
Internal Affairs to become warden at the Central Unit.

Gangs were a major problem and accounted for much of the violence. They fought with each other, with officers, and among themselves.
As the system has identified many gang members and separated them by
transferring to other prison units, the gang leaders found creative ways to
carry on their business involving drugs and "protection" for money, sex,
even supplies from the commissary. Regular mail had been used to give
instructions using codes, sometimes disguised as legal talk. An example
was a letter which targeted Rickie Smith to be killed. It said, "If you happen to run across a dude (interpreted—white boy) by the name of Ricky
(sic) Smith, make sure that Adam Steele (interpreted—homemade prison
knife) talks to him. Smith was a bro (member) at one time but made a
couple of serious mistakes that only Adam can straighten out." Two other
inmates were also targeted in the same letter.

In January 1985, lawyers for the state and inmate attorneys filed an agreed-upon classification plan requiring separation of violent from nonviolent prisoners. That involved much greater use of administrative segregation and ultimately creation of Separate Segregation—SuperSeg. In May, both sides also agreed on a "crowding stipulation." The court ordered that TDC was not to have more than 95 percent of the maximum number of inmates that buildings were designed to house within court guidelines.

That limitation spread the problems of the prisons through the whole criminal justice system. More defendants were being sentenced to prison, but the prison units were filled to the allowable capacity. So the number of paroles granted rose sharply by trying to find inmates who were not inclined to violence and release them to parole supervision. Naturally, the increase in parolees taxed the already stretched parole officers in communities and resulted in less supervision and control of ex-offenders.

Also, county jails around the state were burdened with increased populations because TDC refused to accept new inmates when it would exceed the 95 percent capacity limit. Local jails had to keep newly sentenced prisoners, which increased expenses above what had been budgeted.

Eventually, all these issues awakened citizens and the Texas legislature to take a realistic look at the criminal justice system. The public was naturally concerned with growing crime rates, so relaxing prosecution and sentencing of criminals was not an option. The alternative was to expand the state's ability to incarcerate more felons, which had to be done under the wary and penetrating gaze of Judge William Wayne Justice. All the while, TDC was still trying to hire the officers required to replace the security lost when building tenders were phased out.

The prison system's woes involved more than overcrowding and staffing. A new medical director had been appointed in 1983. Dr. Armond Start came from Oklahoma where he had been head of the medical department of Oklahoma prisons for five years. TDC Director W. J. Estelle could not find a physician in the big State of Texas who would take the job. Start accepted it because, "I like a challenge." It certainly was that. Untrained inmates served as nurses and even physician assistants. Convicts seeking medical attention were typically screened By other inmates. They decided who would see a doctor and sometimes even assisted in surgeries. The president of the National Commission on Health Care, Bernard Harrison, put Texas prisons at the bottom of the list of state systems.

"The conditions are deplorable," he said. Psychiatric care was almost nonexistent, with one full-time psychiatrist and eighteen part-time contractors for 38,000 inmates.

In three years, Dr. Start made great strides in improving health care—another requirement of the federal court orders. The National Commission had accredited more than half the TDC units and others were close to being accredited. Harrison said, "Policies and procedures have been implemented and more staff hired. That doesn't mean they have overcome all their problems. But compared to four years ago, they have done very well."

The turnaround came in spite of serious obstacles. A state budget shortfall brought funding cuts, freezing salaries and preventing the filling of needed staff positions. Also, it was still hard to find competent medical professionals willing to work in the chaos of the prisons, especially at the pay levels offered.

While praised for the significant improvements, Dr. Start was criticized for his leadership style and a grating personality. His reputation was a man who, according to a newspaper article, 'plays by the rules, who does not like mistakes, and who never walks away from a difference of opinion.' "His personality lends itself to making enemies," said Keith Price, who had now become warden of the Darrington Unit. "The problem was his tact—the way he came across. His human relations skills need to be improved." Price also praised Dr. Start for the great strides in improving the medical system, "Despite his poor choice of words, Start's accomplishments speak for themselves."

Dr. Start resigned in the spring of 1986. He said, "I'm tired, worn out. It's time for new blood. I feel exactly as Ray Procunier" (who had recently quit as TDC director, citing burnout.)

Another source for complaints and criticism was the Special Operations Response Team (SORT). Many inmates, besides Rickie Smith, claimed mistreatment by SORT. The teams, to some extent, bridged the gap between the use of inmate 'guards'—building tenders— and the hiring and training of adequate staff for controlling inmates. While regular officers were learning to quit using physical force, SORT would deal with violent inmates, search for weapons and contraband, and intimidate gang members and others who were prone to fighting. The major inmate lockdown of late 1985 and the effectiveness of SORT units greatly reduced the violence in the system.

By 1987, many Special Operations members became regular officers, generally assigned to the Administrative Segregation Blocks and SuperSeg where Rickie and seventeen others were housed and the SORT units were officially disbanded.

Warden Price said, "We still use the concept. We have five-man cell-removal teams. We put the same gear on five big guards and use the same tactics."

Three teams of twelve men remained, renamed Regional Transport Teams, and specializing in escorting dangerous inmates when being moved or taken for court proceedings. Rickie Smith became one of their best customers in a long series of arraignments, trials, and other proceedings.

After SORT was phased out, Warden Jack Garner of the Michael Unit, who had ten SORT-trained officers in the areas where 490 of the more dangerous inmates lived, said, "We got it down well now, and no one gets hurt. This way is actually better because it gives regular officers a chance to be more involved instead of just standing aside and watching someone else do the work." He stated it's harder for inmates to complain against guards, "We don't get that many now. SORT was a good group to blame everything on."

That was another sign that Texas Prisons had largely transitioned from the chaos and violence of the early 1980s to a much smoother operation by 1988. Instead of twenty-four inmate murders in 1984 and twenty-seven in 1985, there were only three or four per year by 1988. Of course it is still prison and some inmates chaffed at being confined and controlled, especially a few, like Rickie Smith, who had built up hatred and bitterness and were not changing their ways. But they were kept in the more secure ways that limited the damage they could do.

The attention of Texas citizens and legislators to the chaos and serious issues brought major change to the prisons. Judge Justice provided an incentive to speed up change at the end of 1986 by finding the Texas Department of Corrections in contempt of court for continued overcrowding—violating his order. He decreed fines of 24 million dollars per month, to begin in three months if inmate living conditions haven't been adjusted.

Just before Justice's contempt citation, Texas voters turned down a second term for Democratic Governor Mark White in favor of Republican William Clements. Prison problems had been a significant issue in the campaign. Before his inauguration in January 1987, Clements met with Judge Justice to pledge that he will get the state in compliance with the court's orders. In February, the legislature and Governor Clements approved an emergency appropriation of 20 million dollars for prisons. In late April, the first month for fines, Justice lifted the contempt finding with no fines assessed. He took the emergency funding as a good sign, so the state was being given some time for the governing process to deal with the problems, but it was obviously on notice that the federal court was watching closely.

That emergency appropriation was just a small start for what would become a massive spending and building effort drastically changing the prison system of Texas. In mid-1985, Texas voters' attitudes were measured in the "Texas Poll," a regular survey conducted by Texas A & M University. Sixty-five percent said "spend more for prisons" and only twenty percent preferred "early release of convicts." Thirty-eight percent felt that prison life was too easy.

The 20 million dollar emergency appropriation of 1987 was followed by a larger budget and then, in the fall, voters approved $500 million in bonds to construct more prisons. Three years later, voters approved another $672 million in bonds to build space for 37,000 new beds. The system operating budget grew from $93 million in 1980 to $621 million in 1990, nearly seven times bigger.

During that same ten years, the average stay in prison was cut almost in half—from 22 months in 1980 to less than 12 months in 1990. Inmates had been serving about half the length of their sentences and went down to serving less than a fifth of their sentences, because of the extreme overcrowding problems. The chairman of the prison board, Charles Terrell, complained that inmates were not incarcerated long enough for any rehabilitation through education, drug and alcohol treatment programs, and other efforts to change behavior. Violent criminals were being released back into society.

In five years after the first bond vote, thirty new prison units were opened and in the next five years fifty-seven more new units were added. The number of inmates in those units also grew amazingly—from about 18,000 in 1980 to 150,000 twenty years later. But the good news was that security improved and violence was more controlled. From that peak of twenty-seven murders in 1985, in 1986 only three homicides occurred and there were between one and five murders in each of the next ten years.

Through the 1980s and into the 1990s, there seemed to be a 'perfect storm' situation in the criminal justice system of Texas. Severe changes in prison operation and prisoner treatment were required by the federal court while the public clamored for more and better law and order. At the same time, many seasoned prison and law enforcement professionals tried to hold on to the traditional ways of dealing with criminals and convicts using force, while others tried to follow the new guidelines to operate in ways that not only were deemed constitutional but also more humane. In the midst of that, there was little in the way of programs for rehabilitation or efforts to help convicts be better citizens when they were released.

CHAPTER TWELVE

Rickie lived in cell #12 in SuperSeg with very few possessions. He had no reading material except for a law book or two, a 3-inch long toothbrush, bar of soap, and usually only one set of clothes—sometimes only boxer shorts.

The normal schedule called for taking each SuperSeg inmate out of the cell for recreation, alone, and a shower, then back in the cell for 23 hours. But normal didn't apply to Rickie. He usually went days or weeks without being taken out of the cell at all. Officers would "shake down" his cell three times a week looking for weapons and contraband. He was always handled roughly and sometimes crowded or even pushed, apparent efforts to provoke him to fight. Often, a guard would pause in front of his cell to make an accusatory or threatening remark, sometimes punctuated with a finger drawn across the throat or simulating shooting Rickie with a pistol.

Other SuperSeg inmates from rival gangs would yell threats and hateful remarks at each other, especially Rickie. Even some from his own gang would make accusations and threats. And, of course, they would throw feces and urine at officers and at each other.

Frequently, Rickie refused his tray of food when officers passed them out. He accused them of putting feces in the food or urinating in the tray. Such mistreatment was testified to by other inmates later in a court hearing. While others experienced some similar treatment, they testified that Rickie got the most and worst ill treatment from guards. Once he discovered small pieces of glass in a cup of coffee.

Either Selestia, his mother, or Becky, long time on and off girlfriend, would come to visit once or twice a month. When the visits were permitted, the hallways from the cell block to the lockdown visitation room would be cleared while he was escorted in cuffs and chains by four officers. The visit was looking through reinforced glass and talking on phone handsets. Many times the visitors would be turned away because officers would not bring Rickie. Also, a lot of mail never got to SuperSeg. Rickie's dad never came to visit.

Of course, Rickie did his part, too—cussing officers, filing complaints, struggling and trying to attack when he could. But the officers were now better trained and extremely wary and careful because they knew Rickie and his reputation very well. So the problems he could cause successfully were not as serious compared to the spearing, stabbing, and breaking out of the cell in mid-1986. That is a summary of how life was for a couple of years.

With day after day locked in a small cell and nothing to divert his attention, Rickie dwelt on himself and his hopeless situation. *Hopeless! I am hopeless*, he said to himself. *My gang brothers are against me. The system is against me. I have no hope. There's no reason for me to try to fix anything or to change.* That reinforced his earlier declarations, *Well, I'll just live down here in prison but I will get respect.*

In that line of thinking, the taunting and threats of the officers served as a form of respect. The cussing and disowning by some Aryan Brotherhood members was validation that he did right by standing up to them for violating their stated principles. However, that didn't really make him feel better, and he was isolated.

He wrote a letter to his mother and declared, "Don't write any more letters to me and don't come to see me anymore. I don't want you to come or write. Forget that I was ever born. Forget that you are my mother."

He sent similar instructions to everyone else he had corresponded with. He said, "I want no ties with you." Of course Selestia paid no attention to those instructions, nor did Becky.

Besides the ongoing hell he was living in, the desperation he felt was deepened by his failure to succeed in attempts to kill a prison guard. Even Officer Crooms had survived the spear going all the way through to his back, although it was a few weeks before Rickie found out he had not died as the warden had told him. A doctor who knew just what to do happened to be at that prison unit at that time and was able to intervene quickly. Doctors were still surprised that Crooms lived.

Added to that was a promise from a prosecuting attorney, "I will see to it that you get a life sentence." Rickie expected that to happen and he would never get out of prison. Now, the goal is to get some respect from his jailers and from the gang enemies.

The daily grind of life in SuperSeg is being interrupted more and more with trips to court hearings and visits from investigators and attorneys from the Special Prosecution Unit, as well as from his own lawyers. There were at least eight state indictments against him for attempted murder and other assaults requiring court appearances. Prosecutors chose to focus on three. Those major crimes occurred in three prisons in three different counties, and the cases had to be handled in courts in each county. There were numerous preliminary hearings related to the three attempted murder cases the state concentrated on: the stabbing of inmate Ross, the spearing of Officer Crooms, and the stabbing of Officer White.

Prosecutors chose to have the actual trial of the most recent attempted murder charge first. That was for stabbing Officer Roger White at the Coffield Unit. A twelve-person jury had been empanelled and prepared to hear the State of Texas versus Rickie Smith in the 349th Judicial District with Judge Melvin D. Whitaker presiding. The wood-paneled courtroom was on the second floor of the historic Anderson County Courthouse on the city square of Palestine, Texas.

Prosecuting attorneys were David Weeks and Travis McDonald of the Special Prison Prosecution Unit. Rickie's court-appointed lawyer was John McDonald—no kin to Travis McDonald on the opposing side.

John McDonald was a veteran defense attorney who early in his career spent six years as a prosecutor, elected county attorney and district attorney, now in private practice.

Trial was to begin at 9:00 AM, May 27, 1987. But before the jury could be brought in, attorneys argued a series of motions before Judge Whitaker. John McDonald made a valiant effort to get the trial delayed and to have one of the prosecutors disqualified, but it was obvious the state's team was in the driver's seat.

The defense had partial success involving the security in the courtroom. He requested removal of the five armed officers in uniform stationed around the courtroom, including one he described as "hovering over the jury box.... I believe this is highly inflammatory and prejudicial to the rights of this defendant to have a fair trial."

Prosecutors countered with a motion to have Rickie kept in physical restraints during the trial. "He is a violent and dangerous individual. We consider him a great threat to the security of the courtroom." He went on to point out there was an attempted murder charge in another county plus two aggravated assault on a correctional officer cases pending against Rickie.

Judge Whitaker ruled that Rickie will be kept in leg irons but without his hands shackled, and the leg irons are not to be displayed before the jury—in the court or even in the hallways. He told the officers to be as "obscure as possible. The court does not want anyone hanging over the jury box."

Then there were technical arguments involving the judge and all attorneys regarding the illness of a juror, whether or not to consider a defense motion to move the trial from Palestine, and a defense request to bring in thirteen other inmates to testify.

The judge ruled the trial will proceed in his courtroom with eleven jurors today. So, an hour-and-a-half late, the jury was brought in. Officer Roger White, the victim, described the stabbing with the 28-inch rod, another officer quoted Rickie as saying, shortly after the incident, "I should have stabbed you, you fat pig." The treating physician testified the wound was 6 inches deep but, miraculously, missed vital organs, "A 6-inch stab is serious and potentially life-threatening." Several witnesses described Rickie as "very dangerous," "violent," "worst of the worst."

The defense attorney suggested White pulled the rod into his abdomen himself in the altercation through the cell door. He also said since the rod struck no organs, the more appropriate charge would be assault, not attempted murder. He gave up on trying to get the thirteen inmates brought from prison to testify that Rickie was mistreated. But he raised the issue of Rickie's mental state. This is in a hearing before the judge without the jury present. John McDonald said that in several meetings, "I have been unable to communicate with him what I thought his defense should be and he has been unable to assist me in the preparation of his defense to the charges herein."

He also brought up that another defense lawyer had "filed an affidavit of insanity as a defense and a motion to have the defendant examined by a psychiatrist."

That was in a preliminary hearing earlier in another county. The motion had been granted, but no examination has ever taken place. Judge Whitaker said he ruled that Rickie is competent to stand trial since all he had in that hearing were attorney's statements. He had asked to talk with Rickie himself, but "Since I was not permitted to inquire of the defendant or talk with him only about that issue, the court overruled the allegation of incompetency to stand trial—on the basis that there was no actual evidence presented to support the allegation." (Whitaker is the judge in Judicial District 349 which covers two counties, so he presided over two trials. Stabbing Officer White was tried in Palestine, Texas, the county seat of Anderson County. The Crooms trial, mentioned at the beginning of chapter one, was in Crockett, Texas, county seat of Houston County.)

The state rested its case and the defense presented no evidence or testimony, but requested the jury instructions include the option of aggravated assault as a verdict. That was overruled. After closing arguments, the jury deliberated eleven minutes and brought a verdict of guilty of attempted capital murder of a prison guard.

Evidence in the punishment phase came from a warden and a prose-cution investigator, both emphasizing how violent and dangerous Rickie Smith was. Then closing arguments. Prosecutors urged assessing the full ninety-nine-year sentence while the defense asked for something between five and twenty years. After another brief meeting, the jury assessed a ninety-nine-year sentence. The trial took less than two days and much of that was lawyer arguments with the jury out of the courtroom.

Rickie was quiet until towards the end when he apparently saw little hope. He shouted things like, "I didn't do it. I didn't do it!" and "I didn't say that. I didn't say that!" and finally, "<u>Why</u> did I do it? <u>Why</u> did I do it?" wanting someone to see that he was defending himself. The judge asked Rickie to be quiet. Finally, he interrupted closing arguments to instruct the jury to disregard Rickie's outbursts. Then, "I'll ask the defen-dant to please remain quiet. If you don't, I'm going to ask you to leave the courtroom." As the jury was dismissed and filing out, Rickie burst out again, "You might as well send me to death row. I'll keep on 'till I kill somebody." Then he looked directly at Investigator Royce Smithey, "Or I'll just kill you."

The stormy finish to the trial was matched by stormy weather outside. About a third of the state, north, central, and eastern areas was covered with strong thunderstorms and sixty-six counties were put under tornado advisories. Graduation ceremonies for schools in counties near the trial in Crockett had to be moved from the stadiums to indoor facilities. The worst damage and flooding caused by the storms occurred about a hun-dred miles away.

Adding ninety-nine years to the ten he was serving confirmed Rickie's feelings of worthlessness and being "absolutely no good!" He assumed he would always remain in prison. He continued causing trouble and sought payback when guards hassled him, but not as effectively as the previous three years, because the officers and the prison operations were better at controlling violence. He still got written up for many infractions like "damaging or destroying property," "refusing to obey," "threaten-ing harm on officer," "possessing contraband," "possessing weapon," "striking an officer," etc. In about five years of this prison term, he had been penalized with loss of 675 days of "good time"—which would have taken almost two years off his original sentence.

Many inmates seem to be able to find a weakness in some of the prison guards and take advantage of it. Even Rickie had calm conversations with some officers. To them it was a welcome break from the hatred and confrontation and it also helped pass the time of an 8-hour shift standing guard over twelve "animals." But often, inmates become very good at 'reading' people. They pick up unintended signals and figure out how to manipulate some officers into doing forbidden favors. It might start with just handing a note to another inmate or some other seemingly simple, harmless thing—then escalate.

Some guards can sympathize with an inmate's difficult situation, real or fabricated, and want to help. Others get into such financial straits that they will take an opportunity for money, even if it means breaking rules. Many inmates can draw on help outside the prison for resources to bribe an officer with such as money, drugs, even sex. Officers have personal lives and can find themselves in family crises or other difficulties which give inmates an opportunity to be a 'friend.' Then, there is old-fashioned blackmail. Get a guy to do simple, little, illegal favors then use that as leverage for more serious lawbreaking.

Rickie was a pretty good con artist when he wanted to be. Among the many officers he crossed paths with during three shifts day after day, week after week, he could find a few he could scam. One might admire his toughness and his commitment to certain principles. Another might sympathize with him for the rough mistreatment he endured from other guards. He had learned and used that skill in the early days when the gangs were almost running some prisons.

All that explanation is to help with understanding how a guy at war with the Texas prison system and described as the most violent inmate ever was able to get drugs and make wine in the most secure cellblock in the whole prison system. Selestia always made sure her "sweet little Rickie" had money for what he needed. She had no idea she helped pay for drugs. Becky, on the other hand, was not only aware but directly involved. She was the primary supplier of drugs, mostly speed and methamphetamines. Sometimes she got them to an officer who would take them inside to Rickie. Sometimes they would be stashed by the fence around the prison perimeter, in the back area on a gravel county road, for an inmate or an officer to pick up and bring inside. Most often, Becky mailed drugs to a post office box and one particular officer picked up and delivered the contraband directly to Rickie in his cell. There was a security camera always trained on the cell block and the cell doors. The officer would throw a blanket over the camera while he opened the bean slot and handed in the drugs.

The wine was made by saving fruits and vegetables and letting them ferment. The process could be speeded up in the winter by getting a guard to take a bag of mix and put it on the radiator for a few hours. Obviously, the result was not even close to wines you buy in nice bottles, but when you get used to the smell and taste you could get drunk—which was the whole idea. Just like for people on the outside, drugs and alcohol provided some diversion from the very difficult life Rickie had made for himself and that diversion was perhaps, sometimes, the motivation for officers to help provide it.

Chapter Thirteen

Rickie's next trial was scheduled for February 1988, just over eight months after the ninety-nine-year sentence for attempted murder of Officer White. This charge is for the attempted murder of inmate Ross three years earlier. That attack occurred at the Diagnostic Unit in Huntsville which is in Walker County. So that's where the trial would be. Trial preparations involved attorneys and investigators for the state and for the defense interviewing people.

There were also court appearances related to the other attempted murder charge for spearing Officer Crooms. Rickie hired an attorney from Houston, Bob Tarrant, to defend him in that case. For his legal fee, he gave Tarrant the motorcycle he wrecked running from police, ending his three months of freedom between prison terms. Insurance repaired the barely used 1983 Harley Davidson Wide Glide and Selestia kept it for Rickie to have when he got out.

The lawyer met Rickie at the Anderson County Courthouse prior to a preliminary hearing on the attempted murder charge. Rickie was obviously drunk from his homemade wine. He was little help with a legal defense.

"How do you get drunk in prison?" Tarrant blurted.

Rickie just grinned and didn't explain.

"You've got to act sober before the judge. Besides, you have no case—too many offenses and no defense." In the hearing, a not guilty plea was entered but no defense was presented.

Later, Tarrant entered the motion for a sanity hearing, claiming Rickie was mentally incapable of defending himself legally. This was the filing referenced at the first trial in chapter twelve. The motion said, "The defendant has a prolonged history of unusual, unexplainable, bizarre behavior ... beginning soon after his incarceration ... until the present." It also suggested "deterioration of his mental faculties ... significant, sudden personality changes." It continued citing Rickie's "belief that everyone, including prison guards and inmates, is trying to kill him, yet he cannot give any reason for his belief. His inability to carry on an intelligent conversation and discuss his legal problems in a coherent manner has grown progressively worse in the last few months." The motion states that unless he is sent to a mental hospital and examined by psychiatrists, "the defendant will be denied due process of law" violating the US Constitution.

District Judge Whitaker granted the motion for the psychiatric examination, but as mentioned in chapter 12, Rickie was never taken to a mental institution or evaluated by mental health personnel.

Attorney Tarrant was unreliable, not showing up for court hearings and doing little in interviewing Rickie and others to prepare a defense. He did talk to Assistant Warden Michael Upshaw who said, "Inmate Smith is probably the most violent inmate I've dealt with in twelve-and-a-half years. He is a very cold person without regards for human life. He doesn't care whether he lives another day or whether you live another day. He has to be as close to the devil of anybody I've ever dealt with."

The lawyer kept telling Rickie he has no case, "You are a loser." Finally, he quit as the defense attorney, citing health problems. He suffered from hepatitis which Rickie was sure came from needles while using drugs. His leaving the case probably helped the question of Rickie's mental state slip through the cracks.

Tarrant's case for a mental examination might have been helped by some careful observation of Rickie's behavior day to day. He would sleep no more than 4 or 5 hours at a time, waking up in a rage. It would begin as hatred of certain officers and expand to the whole prison system and then include some of the convict enemies. But, frequently, the hatred became bitterness and frustration with himself and his situation. He hated what he had become and he was discouraged that he has not succeeded in killing anyone from the Texas Department of Corrections. Sometimes he really wanted to die, but any thought of suicide was quickly dismissed because, "I will not give all these people the satisfaction of seeing me carried out in a plastic bag." Besides, his hatred would not let him give up in this war with his enemies.

The charge of trying to kill inmate Ross came to trial February 16, 1988 in Huntsville, in Walker County. Hal Ridley was the court-appointed defense attorney. Mark Patterson of the Special Prison Prosecution Office represented the state. Judge Allen Stilley presided. Eight women and four men were selected for the jury.

This trial went pretty fast, like the first one nine months before. Witnesses from the Walker County Sheriff's Office and from the prison system described how Rickie bolted from the line of nearly naked prisoners, pushed the sheriff aside, and stabbed inmate Ross with the "shank"—homemade knife. He was trying to carry out the "hit" on Ross that had been ordered by Aryan Brotherhood bosses. There was no defense testimony. The jury took less than an hour to find him guilty and only 15 minutes to set sentence at the maximum ninety-nine years. The verdicts came on February 18, 1988—a memorable date for what came next.

Becky was in the courtroom each day for the trial, just as she had been in the previous trial and sometimes even for brief preliminary court hearings. She took all opportunities to see Rickie, though it was just from the audience with no chance to talk.

Unknown to Rickie, Becky talked with Judge Stilley before the trial. When it was concluded and the jury dismissed, the judge said the defendant, Rickie, could talk to Becky. She leaned over the rail in front of the audience benches and announced to Rickie that the judge had agreed to marry them.

"What?" Rickie blurted. "Why? I'll never get out of prison. This is crazy, isn't it, gal?"

"I don't care," Becky said. "They can't take this away from us. They've taken everything else."

"I just got ninety-nine more years," Rickie protested.

"It's the least you can do," Becky retorted.

"Fine!" Rickie surrendered. "If that's what you want."

The court bailiff and two prison guards led Rickie, in handcuffs and leg chains, to stand in front of the judge's bench and Becky came through the swinging doors of the railing to stand beside them. One guard took a step back and Becky moved over against Rickie. It was a very brief ceremony. Judge Stilley asked Rickie, "Do you, Rickie Andrew Smith, take this woman to be your lawful wedded wife?"

Rickie replied with a halfhearted "Yes."

The judge turned, "And, do you Becky Lykens, take this man to be your lawful wedded husband?"

"I do," Becky exclaimed, beaming.

"You may kiss," he instructed.

They did, but it was mostly Becky kissing Rickie who was hampered by handcuffs.

Judge Stilley proclaimed, "This request has been brought before the court. It's crazy, but I pronounce you man and wife." He looked around the room, smiled, and said, "I have never before sentenced a man to ninety-nine years in prison and then married him off."

The prison officers grabbed Rickie's arms and led him away, pulling him out of the hold Becky had on his cuffed hands. They returned him to his single cell number 12 in SuperSeg while Becky went home to Houston. With the 2-minute "honeymoon" over, life went back to the routine of the most secure cell block in the prison system.

Soon, prosecutors were proceeding with building their case against Rickie on the charge of attempted murder of Officer Kervin Crooms at the

Eastham Unit in May 1986. That trial will be in Crockett, Texas, county seat of Houston County in November of '88. A court-appointed attorney, Neil Durrance of Crockett, took over from the Houston lawyer Rickie had hired but later quit. Mark Patterson of the Special Prison Prosecution Unit led the state's team as in the Huntsville trial. The investigator for the prosecution team, Royce Smithey, had been involved in preparations for the two previous trials and Rickie had built up a real dislike for him. To Smithey, Rickie was just another of many incorrigible inmates he dealt with. However, he noticed that Rickie became more belligerent in each trial. It caught his attention that Rickie never showed any remorse. "When the juries would come back with a guilty verdict, he showed no remorse at all," Smithey said. "His eyes were—well, it was kind of like looking into a shark's eyes, just lifeless, dead."

On the other hand, Smithey was impressed with Rickie's reputation for loyalty to friends and to principles he held to, like the ones he accused his gang leaders of violating. He would do anything for those who respected him. "Several inmates would constantly tell me, 'You don't know the real Rickie. All you see is an animal that's being caged up that somebody's always picking at.'" The investigator figured out, "If you disrespect him, then he has no feelings for you whatsoever, but he is always loyal and will fight for those who are loyal to him."

Becky came regularly to visit Rickie—as did Selestia, his mother—and for appearances in court. Also, she kept a steady supply of drugs coming as well as using them herself. Someone told her about Hospitality House where she could spend the night free and save motel costs when court proceedings lasted more than one day. Hospitality House was two blocks from what then was the headquarters building for the Texas Department of Criminal Justice and the original state prison, the Walls Unit in Huntsville. It is sponsored by the Texas Baptist Convention as a ministry to families coming to visit inmates in the many prison units in the Huntsville area. There were motel-type rooms. Meals were not served, but snacks and some canned goods were usually available for guests to fix for themselves. More contact between families and inmates generally helped keep the family from disintegrating.

When Becky was going to Hospitality House, Bob and Nelda Norris, the original directors, were there. They would spend evenings visiting with guests who were willing to talk. They wanted them to feel welcome and even did some counseling with those who were emotionally stressed in their circumstances. It's well known that most inmate families have emotional, financial, social, and other difficulties. Becky, often on drugs, was comforted by the interest and compassion of the Norrises. She also was upset by the constant anger and bitterness expressed by Rickie.

One evening, she was chatting with Bob Norris in the large commons room. She found herself explaining that she felt so bad because she can't help Rickie. "Maybe you can talk to him," she pleaded. "Please, see if you can help him. He is so unhappy. So bitter and angry. He's not the same man I used to know. I love him and it hurts so much to see him like this."

Bob tried to console her, "Well, I'll see what I can do." Bob knew he couldn't visit unless the inmate had agreed and put him on his visitor's list. *And why would he put me, a stranger, on the list?* he thought. His next thought was, *What can I say to the most violent inmate in prison who just got another ninety-nine-year sentence?*

Becky, too, knew it was unlikely Rickie would talk to anyone. But she told him about this very nice man who may get in touch with him. "He has been helpful to me and I asked him to talk to you." They both figured that was the end of it.

Shortly after 6:00 AM, November 2, 1988, eight men in battle fatigues and flak jackets came to Rickie's cell. The sergeant of the group ordered Rickie to remove his clothes, then had him turn around and around. He handed his clothing out through the bean slot to be searched. The clothes were passed back for him to put on while several pair of eyes watched. Next Rickie backed up to the open slot with his hands behind his back where they were handcuffed. It's a routine quite familiar to Rickie and all the other convicts in SuperSeg. Somewhere on the cell block a radio was playing Michael Jackson singing "Man in the Mirror."

The big door was opened and Rickie took two steps. A heavy chain was locked around his waist and shackles were secured around each ankle. Finally, a chain was locked to the leg shackles, the belly chain, and the handcuffs. He could raise his hands only a few inches and take smaller than normal steps. Surrounded by the eight men of the Special Transport Team, he shuffled out of SuperSeg and down the long hallway of the Coffield Prison to the back door, stopping at each door to wait for the men to make sure no one else was close and for the door to be unlocked electronically. He was escorted to the Special Transport Van and put in the middle seat. Two others in combat attire were waiting in the front seat of the van. Two of the escorts got in behind Rickie, the rest went to two other vehicles. One led the van and the other followed.

The convoy waited for the chain-link gate to be unlocked and opened, then proceeded to Farm to Market Road #2054. It sped through the almost ghost town of Tennessee Colony and onto US Highway 287 and headed eighteen miles to Palestine. It was barely daylight when the vehicles pulled into the city square and stopped in front of the courthouse. Some officers, carrying assault rifles, got out and blocked all traffic on that side of the square and waved pedestrians away from the sidewalk to the building. Then they surrounded Rickie and escorted him into the building, up a flight of stairs, past the courtroom and into a small anteroom, to await the time to go into the courtroom. His attorney, Neal Durrance, was permitted to come in, sit at the table, and talk with his client. Judge Melvin Whitaker, who presided at the first trial in Crockett, was also the presiding judge here in the adjoining County of Houston.

This was a very contentious trial. The prosecution bolstered the reputation that Rickie was the most violent man in prison, while his young defense attorney tried valiantly but largely unsuccessfully, to get before the jury that prison staff routinely threatened, harassed, and actually mistreated the inmate. It appeared to be an attempt to show that the spearing of Officer Crooms was a type of "preventive self-defense" action. But since no testimony or evidence showed any direct threat to Rickie at the time of the spearing, Judge Whitaker would not allow the jury hear about the numerous other conflicts that were brought up. Durrance subpoenaed many prison inmates to tell about times they saw officers mistreat Rickie. But Judge Whitaker required them to tell what they saw to him and on the court record, but excluded their testimony before the jury because they were not talking about the time that Crooms was stabbed. He allowed the testimony in the record so Durrance would have it in case an appeals court gave it relevance and viewed it differently than he did. (The appeals court did not.)

There was no substantive dispute over the basic facts that Rickie Smith used the spear and that officer Crooms was critically wounded. The most attention in the trial centered on how much danger Rickie posed to people in the courtroom if he was not kept in the maximum constraints possible. That debate delayed the start of the trial, as described in chapter one, and then came up again late in the afternoon of the second day. Rickie complained of pain in his hands and wrists which were immobilized by the metal box secured to them and to the handcuffs. His attorney spoke to the judge who then dismissed the jury for the day.

Durrance then listed the restraints—"steel handcuffs with a box and a chain which goes through the gird belt and also with some leg chains as well. He has sat—it's been 12 hours now. It was approximately 18 hours yesterday. I can see from his hands they are irritated and beginning to swell." He said the defendant asked to speak to the judge about it.

Judge Whitaker agreed and Rickie became a sworn witness for the purpose of having it in the trial record:

"Question. Are you having trouble with your hands?

Answer: Yes, I am. They are swelling up, and they're hurting. They are red and irritated. They are not bleeding yet, but they've got red marks all over both my arms. If I've got to continue to sit here like this, I'd just soon the judge exclude me and try me and leave me in my cell if I've got to wear these boxes.

Q. For the benefit of the record....

A. Due to my pain that I'm suffering, that's what I'm requesting.

Q. Is it painful for you to remain seated?

A. Yes, it is.

Q. And is it painful for your hands to remain with your arms partially crossed and separated?

A. Yes. There is no way to move them nowhere. Sitting here for the amount of hours that I've sat here, it's uncomfortable to the point that it's painful, and I don't want to be here no more."

Of course, the restraints were put on early in the morning for the inmate to come out of his cell and were not removed until he was locked in a cell for the night.

Prosecutor Mark Patterson recalled James Glissom, the TDC officer in charge of securing and transporting the inmate. Glissom reiterated that it would be dangerous to remove any of the restraints, "The Bureau of Classification recommended that he was not to be let out of the cell unless all mechanical restraints were placed on inmate Smith. He has been involved in numerous staff assaults and—I'm not sure, I would have to review—I believe inmate assaults. He's had a history of weapons. He's not to be placed where he can get his hands on anything that could be fashioned into a weapon."

Q. "Is he also classified as an escape risk?"

A. "Yes, sir."

Further questioning brought out that there is no way to know if someone might pass a potential weapon to the defendant and that he could perhaps get a paper clip from the table and pick the lock of his handcuffs if his hands were not secure.

Finally, Judge Whitaker declared, "The restraints are continued. The law provides that if a defendant voluntarily absents himself after pleading to the indictment, which he has done, or after the jury has been selected, which has happened, in a trial before a jury, the trial may proceed to its conclusion without the presence of the defendant. If he doesn't want to come tomorrow, I want to put it on the record now." He then asked the defense attorney, "Are you sure that's what you want?"

Durrance replied, "No, sir."

"Is that what he wants?"

Rickie proclaimed, "Yes, sir, because of the box. My hands are swelling up. I can't wear this stuff no longer. I'm not going to sit here!"

There was more discussion with the defense attorney telling Rickie that he needed his help with certain defense witnesses as he would have to go forward with the case. Rickie told the lawyer to forget the case, but Durrance said he will proceed with it to the best of his ability. After several more declarations that he did not want to be there, court was recessed. The judge gave Glissom his home number so he could call him the next morning to say whether Rickie still declined to be in the trial.

Rickie did not change his mind and was not taken to the courtroom. But his lawyer made a valiant effort to show that Rickie's behavior was directly related to mistreatment by prison staff. Before the jury was brought into court, Durrance asked reconsideration of the denial of a motion for certain witnesses to appear.

"In support thereof, I will tender to the court at this time an affidavit signed and notarized by Elisio Martinez reciting certain facts concerning an Officer Joe Moss and the defendant in this case, Rickie Smith, involving a direct attempt on his life."

Judge, "Your motion will be denied. You can mark that whatever number you want that is appropriate, not for the jury's view but for the record purposes."

Durrance again brought up the motion to have Rickie brought in without the "black box."

"How many times am I going to have to rule on that? The ruling of the court will stand." The judge then revealed to the attorneys that he had received a letter from Rickie after the previous trial he presided over, stabbing inmate Ross, in which he repeated his threats to keep on until he killed someone and got on death row. Judge Whitaker also had been advised by the FBI that an informant said Whitaker was on an Aryan

Brotherhood hit list. He said that shook him up enough that he started sleeping with the lights on and notified local law enforcement agencies of the threats. That relates to the extraordinary security involved in bringing Rickie to this trial and the supposed plan to ambush the prison convoy on the Brazos River bridge as mentioned in chapter one.

The defense case consisted of inmates and officers being asked about various incidents of mistreatment of Rickie by staff. Over and over guards and supervisors denied all accusations or claimed no knowledge or memory of the alleged incidents. Apparently there were no reports of them in the prison records either. Most of those witnesses were not before the jury.

One typical exchange was with an Officer Hardin, called as a defense witness.

"Q. During the month of May of 1986, did you know an inmate by the name of Rickie Smith?

A. Yes, sir, I did…. I believe I did some notary work for him and assisted him by bringing his law books to his cell.

Q. During that period of time, did he ever discuss his situation with you there at the Texas Department of Corrections?

A. Not to my recollection.

Q. Do you recall whether or not he ever told you that his life was threatened?

A. No, sir.

Q. Do you recall whether or not he ever said that his life was in danger?

A. No, sir….

Q. Do you recall an incident involving Officer Crooms and Mr. Smith in May of 1986?

A. Yes, sir.

Q. Do you recall a conversation with Mr. Smith in the law library approximately two to three days prior to that incident when he talked with you for about an hour stating that he felt that his life was in danger, that he was being threatened, and he was being placed in an untenable position?

A. No, sir.

Q. I may not have used—he may not have used those words, but he felt that he was threatened.

A. Not that I recall.

Q. You don't remember that?

A. No, sir.

Q. Did Mr. Smith ever discuss with you any problems concerning his treatment by the guards or any of the employees of TDC?

A. No, sir, not that I recall.

Another interesting exchange was with Sergeant Joe Moss. After establishing that the sergeant worked in SuperSeg for a while and knowing inmate Smith, the defense attorney asked about two other inmates who Moss denied having any connection with. (One had given the affidavit Durrance put on the record about Moss.) Then came:

"Q. Do you recall approaching them concerning the possibility of making a hit on Mr. Smith?

A. No, sir. I was investigated by Internal Affairs, but that was not true. That conversation never existed.

Q. It never took place?

A. No, sir.

Q. You don't remember making an offer of drugs or magazines?

A. No, sir.

Q. You never told them you would leave the door open?

A. No, sir. That's not the truth.

Q. And it was investigated by Internal Affairs, was it not?

A. Yes, sir.

Q. And you were moved from the Coffield Unit after that, is that correct?

A. I was moved from the Coffield Unit when I made sergeant at the Mark W. Michael Unit.

Q. Was Mr. Smith, in your opinion, a problem when he was on the Coffield Unit?

A. Yes, sir. He's threatened me on three different occasions.

Q. Did you dislike Mr. Smith?

A. I worked with him in a professional manner....

Q. Was a grievance filed against you as a result of this incident in the Coffield Unit?

A. I don't recall, but I think there was."

All the side issues, technical legal arguments, objections, motions for a mistrial and frequent moving the jury in and out of the courtroom did not distract the panel from unanimously voting "guilty." They deliberated less than an hour and then hardly took 15 minutes to assess the maximum ninety-nine years. The third such sentence in eighteen months.

Through the three days of the trial, the defense attorney made more than fifty motions for a mistrial and all were denied. A number of times Judge Whitaker explained that other events in the prison may need attention, but in this trial only activities related to the stabbing of Officer Crooms were to be considered. The Fifth Circuit Court of Appeals panel agreed. Reviewing the complete record, not just what the jury heard, the verdict and sentence were upheld.

But the implication of testimony and questions related to the turmoil and conflict surrounding inmate Rickie Smith is that it was not a one-sided war. Judge Whitaker seemed to acknowledge that, but knew that under the law one wrong act does not justify another wrong act.

So, in late 1988, Rickie Smith had been in Texas prisons long enough to have been paroled from the ten-year sentence he began with but was now facing almost 300 more years in prison. It was likely he would spend as many of those years that he lived in the most secure and most uncomfortable part of what had become one of the largest state prison system in the country.

CHAPTER FOURTEEN

An officer strolled down the row of cells in SuperSeg, occasionally stopping just long enough to hand the inmate in a cell his mail. His last delivery was a letter for Rickie Smith in cell 12, at the end of the cell block. This is in December 1988, about a month after getting his third ninety-nine-year prison sentence. He didn't recognize the name Bob Norris on the return address as he opened the envelope. The letter began with the explanation that he was writing at the request of Becky Smith. She had talked with him when she stayed at Hospitality House during the recent trial. He had seen the newspaper report of the trial and how much prison time had piled up and he had heard how bitter, angry, and unhappy Rickie was.

Norris wrote that the purpose of the letter was to tell Rickie that Jesus Christ loves him and wants to give him peace. He wrote that he has been praying for Rickie and wants him to receive Christ for salvation.

"Ha," Rickie sniffed as he folded the letter and stuck it in a little bag of letters, "how many times have I heard that crap?"

Soon another letter arrived from Norris. It said, "God wants to give you peace. Jesus has a plan for your life. He wants to set you free." Rickie read it out loud to convicts in other cells and said, "Hey, guys, don't worry about all those long prison sentences, God wants to set you free." Other inmates then joined in cussing and making fun of God and about how He can set them free from this rotten prison.

Every few weeks another letter came from Norris. Sometimes, Rickie would even look up a scripture that was mentioned, but they never made sense to him. Then he would tear up the letter and scatter it out in the cell block. Finally, he wrote back to Norris and asked, "What's your real objective for writing me all these stinking letters? I can't understand. You must not have nothing to do with your time. What's your REAL reason for this?"

Norris wrote back to say the letters were not HIS objective, it was the Holy Spirit's purpose to give him peace. That really set Rickie off. He tore the letter in twenty or thirty tiny pieces as he thought, *That's exactly what I need, peace*. But that was the farthest thing away, *and I don't want to hear it*. He wrote Norris demanding he stop writing.

Meanwhile, life went on as usual. One day, he was drinking his homemade wine and a man from some ministry group came to talk with whoever would let him. When he got to cell 12 Rickie offered him wine. "Jesus turned water to wine, too. Would you like some of mine?" He mocked Jesus and cursed the visitor, who left.

When he wasn't drunk or high on drugs, Rickie's rage continued and his depression grew worse. He was feeling especially bad because his wife was arrested for smuggling drugs into the prison for him. Becky and three prison guards were charged with delivering Tylenol 4, Valium, and speed to inmate Rickie Smith, described in the indictment as a member of the white supremacist Aryan Brotherhood prison gang. (Tylenol 4 contains codeine, a controlled substance.) The Special Prosecution Unit said Becky Smith was filling prescriptions and mailing the drugs to the guards. One guard was being paid with drugs. Travis McDonald, of the Special Prosecution Unit, said, "It's outrageous to me that guards would bring drugs in to someone who's stabbed two other guards."

The crime was discovered in an unexpected and interesting way. One of Rickie's gang brothers had a girlfriend named Linda whom he had introduced to Becky at some point. The women became friends and Linda was at Becky's one time when Becky prepared a package of drugs to mail to the officer. What Becky didn't know was that Linda was an informant for the Texas Rangers investigators. She called the Rangers with the information and they began surveillance which resulted in arrests of Becky and the three guards. Becky and an officer were each sentenced to ten years in prison, although Becky actually served only a year and a half.

"I feel as low as a snake because I drew her into this," Rickie told a neighbor. When Becky went to prison, of course, that removed most of his supply of drugs for a while. Also, the guards who had been willing to help Rickie cook his wine became more cautious.

What Rickie "drew Becky into" was actually way more than smuggling some drugs into prison. The Aryan Brotherhood had a thriving business outside of prison. Becky became a contact person. Mostly, she would pick up convicts when they were released and take them to Brotherhood brothers. There was a "chop-shop" where stolen cars and trucks would be altered and given new titles. Many became the ex-cons vehicles and were used in all kinds of crimes which brought in money for use on the outside and for supplying drugs and money to AB members inside. Becky became part of the Brotherhood to the extent she had money and whatever else she needed. Of course, her part came to a screeching halt with her arrest and prison sentence.

Rickie became more agitated and depressed. His mother, Selestia, still came to visit frequently, although often, she was turned away because officers refused to bring Rickie out of his cell.

Prison life in SuperSeg stayed pretty much the same. A few inmates were moved in or out, but they were all still gang leaders and extremely violent offenders and often they had a grudge against the "famous" Rickie Smith.

On March 27, 1989, the Twelfth Circuit Court of Appeals issued a ruling that upheld the conviction verdict in the attempted murder trial and the ninety-nine-year prison sentence for stabbing inmate Ross. That's just another of many events that caused Rickie to hate the system and to despise himself.

The week before, the same appellate court had ruled that the trial court had erred in the case against Rickie for stabbing Officer White, two-and-a-half years earlier. The defense attorney, John McDonald, had moved to have Rickie examined for competency to stand trial. Judge Whitaker denied that motion because he had no evidence to consider and he had not been permitted to meet with Rickie himself. The conviction in that case was appealed as a matter of routine. A new court-appointed attorney, William House, filed the appeal and cited the competency issue.

The appellate court said such an issue raised during a trial brings an obligation for the trial court to "assay just that evidence tending to show incompetency, putting aside all competing indications of competency, to find whether there is some evidence, a quantity more than none or a scintilla, that rationally may lead to a conclusion of incompetency." It ruled that if competency at the trial date cannot be determined, a new trial is to be granted.

McDonald had actually called himself as a witness to testify that Rickie had been unable to assist him in preparation of his defense. He also cited the motion for an insanity defense another attorney had made in a pretrial hearing, which was never dealt with.

McDonald's testimony was quoted in the appeal that was filed in the stabbing of Officer White. The appellate court remanded the case to the trial court to determine if the defendant's competency at the time of trial can now be determined. A week later the same court upheld the conviction in the Ross trial where mental state was first raised but not in the actual trial.

Seven months later, October 17, 1989, a competency trial was held with Judge R. W. Lawrence presiding.

A psychologist explained the difficult process to try to determine competency two-and-a-half years later. Then several inmates were brought in to testify, hoping to show that Rickie was especially mistreated by officers and paranoid to the point of not being able to deal with matters rationally. The first said that in SuperSeg, "there was continual harassment, officers claiming that they was putting something in our food, name-calling about the cases that we were back there behind."

Then he said, "Officers would come to our cell and tell us things about Rickie Smith and it was kind of like them wanting to justify their reason for harassing Rickie Smith. He acted as though he was paranoid, watching everybody. He appeared to be scared of things that other inmates didn't think he had reason to be."

The defense attorney asked, "Was he imagining things?"

"I would say that some of the things were happening but they weren't as bad as he may have thought it was and some of them just wasn't happening at all."

The attorney asked about guards tampering with food on the trays they brought Rickie and the inmate said he couldn't say he actually saw them mess with Rickie's tray, but he saw them do things to some trays, "such as urinating in their tray or spitting in the tray."

When asked about discussing his case, "Rickie would talk about it, then he would go off onto something else. He would never get on one main subject and stay on it."

Of course, there were many objections by the state's attorney to the inmate's testimony.

Rickie's wife, Becky, was called to testify.

"How would you describe Rickie during your visits preceding May of '87?"

"He was scared, real scared; paranoid, scared, in fear for his life."

The state brought out that Becky was in prison for smuggling drugs to Rickie. She said she was supposed to be released that day—having finished her sentence.

Then came inmate Jeff Lykens, who had tried to kill Rickie on orders from Aryan Brotherhood leaders. He was also in SuperSeg. He said there was constant harassment by officers.

"Can you be specific toward Rickie?"

"I observed a officer putting feces in the ventilation duct behind Smith's cell. I observed an officer urinating in Smith's tray. I observed several different officers at different occasions making threatening gestures towards Smith, like running their finger across their throat or acting like they had a gun pointed at him and pulling the trigger. I've had occasion to witness officers verbally threaten him."

Asked if he tried to help Rickie prepare his defense, Lykens said, "He would comprehend when I was talking to him, but then like a few hours later it was like I hadn't even told him anything at all." His testimony concluded with, "He was under so much stress. He didn't know about the law. He wasn't educated in the law and he was having—the only thing he would do is just have verbal outbursts, displays of anger, things like that."

Another inmate was called but he refused to testify, "Due to the hostility that's been experienced from my point of transfer all the way up here by the officials of the Texas Department of Corrections, I'm not going to testify in this trial without the court's assurance that there will not be any retaliation for my testimony." With the jury out of the room, he said he saw many times that Smith was being set up by officers, like planting a knife behind the cell where Smith could not get. Asked how Rickie handled it, he said, "He was paranoid, he was losing touch with reality ... and it got to the point to where it was just impossible to communicate with him." But he would not testify before the jury.

Then came the attorney, John McDonald, who represented Rickie in the trial and requested a competency examination. "It was very difficult to communicate with him because he seemed entirely and completely involved with his paranoid ideas about the threats he felt to his life from both the guards and—you know, he was preoccupied with this."

On cross examination, the state's attorney accused McDonald of being incompetent by not filing formal motions on incompetency instead of just bringing it up during the trial. That brought the revelation that the defense was led to believe there would be no trial because the state wanted to get Rickie transferred to some other prison out of the state of Texas, which did not happen.

Finally, the state's only evidence was testimony from a prison warden, who was an assistant warden at Coffield when Rickie went to trial. He testified that he had many meetings with Rickie on various violations and charges and that he always discussed them rationally and showed no sign of incompetency or not understanding. The case then went to the jury for deliberations. They returned a verdict of no evidence of incompetency at the time of the trial two-and-a-half years earlier. While this does not change anything legally, it does give a fairly graphic picture of how life was for Rickie Smith during several years in Super Segregation at the Texas Department of Criminal Justice. Obviously, there was a two-sided war going on. And with no ruling of incompetency, the appeals court denied the appeal of ninety-nine years on the attempted murder conviction.

The new ways of prison operation were finally taking hold in the late 1980s. There still were some who held onto the old ways of handling inmates. But so many new officers had been hired and trained under the new federal court guidelines that it had become the new normal. Discipline was mostly through formal processes rather than physical use of force and intimidation.

Being a prison guard is a difficult job. There's constant anxiety knowing that at any time you can be verbally assaulted or even physically attacked and that other than immediate defense against serious danger, you cannot react physically. You must develop a "thick skin" and ignore threats and deal with attacks through proper channels.

Many inmates appreciated the new regulations and inmate-officer relations were much more bearable—even appreciated. But there were always "tough guys" and those who couldn't stand restrictions of prison rules. The difficulty of the job was multiplied in the administrative segregation cell blocks and especially in Super Segregation that was created for what a former prison director called "the cream of the crud." Many officers assigned to SuperSeg would transfer to other jobs because of the stress. Finally, the administration made those assignments permanent to try to establish more continuity. Guards would learn just how much retaliation against the troublemakers they could get away with and there were some who, by nature, fitted into the job of dealing with the really bad guys like Rickie Smith. Others would just give up and quit or be fired. And a few would bend some rules to get along with inmates—as mentioned earlier about Rickie making wine and getting drugs.

Rickie was puzzled by one notable exception to how officers handled SuperSeg convicts, an officer named Carl Robinson. Rickie had tried his best to kill five guards and when the security finally made that nearly impossible, he would entertain himself by intimidating them. His reputation helped him put fear into the officers. But Robinson was not intimidated. He showed no fear when Rickie tried and that frustrated him greatly. One of the rules they made for Rickie was that he had to stand at the back of his cell with his hands on the back wall while his meals were put into the cell. If he refused he did not eat. But when Robinson was bringing food he paid no attention to where Rickie was—even standing by the door, sometimes even turned his back to the cell with the "bean slot" door open. It would have been easy to run a knife or a spear through the slot and into the guard—as he had done before. He also noticed that Robinson would look him in the eye, unlike most officers. So he asked why he was not concerned about Rickie stabbing him.

Robinson replied, "Well, Rickie, if you want to stab someone, I would rather you stab and kill me than one of these other officers that don't know Jesus or know where they'll spend eternity."

That infuriated Rickie who cussed Robinson out and said, "I'm not the crazy one—you are." He continued ranting while Robinson calmly walked down the cell block, which prompted more raving and cursing. Robinson treated the other SuperSeg inmates with the same calm even when urine was thrown on him.

One day an attorney involved in monitoring compliance with federal court orders came into SuperSeg. She looked in various cells and asked a few questions of inmates. She saw a chain and extra lock on the door of Rickie's cell and looked inside noticing there was no mattress on the concrete bunk. She asked about it and he said, "Lady, I've had no mattress for six months. They won't give me one."

She asked why.

"They hate me! I haven't been to recreation in more than a year, and the only shower I get is a goon pulling the fire hose down here and shooting it into the cell."

Not sure whether to believe him or not, she checked with other inmates and some guards, concluding that Rickie was telling the truth.

She left but quickly returned with the Coffield warden. The cell was opened and the warden personally put handcuffs on Rickie, then had an officer put a new mattress on the bunk.

Apparently, when she left she sent an urgent report to Judge William Wayne Justice. Soon, TDC officials were in court to be told such treatment is not acceptable. He was told that there was no dayroom for SuperSeg inmates to have indoor recreation in bad weather. He ordered one built and threatened them with jail if it wasn't done in ninety days. A severe winter storm blew in after construction started with near zero temperatures, much too cold for concrete work. A temporary shelter was built around the site so space heaters could make it warm enough to continue work. The threats of Judge Justice were taken seriously enough to not wait for warmer weather. This was also an embarrassment because TDC had claimed that all inmates had access to indoor and outdoor recreation.

After the project was done and in use, Rickie saw the warden in the cell block. He told him loudly, with a big grin, that he greatly appreciated his providing the dayroom. The warden's face turned red and he stalked out. Rickie felt that the lawyer's intervention kept him from suddenly turning up dead.

Sometime later, a neighbor of Rickie named Tony Rice was involved in the trial of his life. A new law was passed that if a gang member was convicted of killing another inmate, it was a capital murder crime punishable by execution. Rice was the first one to be charged under that law. He was a leader of the Texas Mafia Gang. He was Rickie's nearest neighbor, two cells away. (The cell next to him was kept empty and he was in the last cell on the row to keep him isolated, because of previous escapes from his cell.) Rice chose to be his own attorney in the murder trial, which was in its third day, and he was extremely frustrated with how it seemed to be going. So he was loudly proclaiming his anger, cursing God, ranting at the prison, denouncing the laws, and anything that came to mind. His bean slot was open for chow and he slung a Bible through the slot and it slid across the floor.

About that time, Rickie was being taken out to shower and he stopped in front of Rice's cell to say, "Why are you letting that book upset you so much? It's nothing but paper and ink, written by men to control people. Wouldn't it make more sense to be working on your legal strategy, reading a law book or something besides ranting and cussing an ol' book that's nothing but ink and paper?" Then the escorts moved him on to the shower.

Carl Robinson was hearing all this and while Rickie was in the shower, he picked up the Bible and put it in Rickie's cell. When he returned from the shower, got the handcuffs taken off and the bean slot locked, he noticed the Bible. He knew who put it there, so he grabbed it and headed to the cell door to yell at Robinson. Then it dawned on him that he had just told Rice it was a harmless book written by men and it would appear hypocritical if he showed anger about it. So he chunked it to the back of his cell.

And so went life in SuperSeg. It was populated with quite a mixture of the good, the bad, and the ugly. Sometimes you couldn't tell one from the other. But after Rickie's incompetency trial and other events during the same time, he was even more depressed. (Those events are in Chapter Fifteen.) He knew what most officers thought of him and that many inmates would be glad to have the opportunity to kill him, but listening to all the things his supposed friends said about him in the trial made him even more convinced than ever that he was worthless and had no hope of changing anything. He had over 300 years of prison sentence built up so obviously there was no hope of ever getting out. He had tried to kill guards and inmates without success. He despised the day-to-day existence he was in. There was absolutely no value or happiness in his life and he saw no way to change that. He knew that his mother and Becky were the only people who cared anything about him and he just caused them hurt. Sometimes he daydreamed back to when he and Tippy would walk through the woods or get in the boat and go fishing, but then was jolted to reality by some convict outburst or a commotion with the guards and knows that he would never have that peace again. He couldn't even escape into sleep. When he finally wore out enough to get to sleep, in no more than 4 hours he was jolted awake by anger, hatred, frustration, and all those thoughts of hopelessness. He was only animated by some threat or conflict that got some adrenaline flowing. Life was not worth living.

Meanwhile, the Texas Department of Criminal Justice had been dealing with even bigger problems. In 1980 the system had grown to 30,000 inmates. They were spread out in eighteen prison units. As 1989 drew to a close there were thirty-seven, twice as many prisons in ten years. The number of officers had also doubled to 10,500, and the inmate population had almost doubled to over 51,000. The building boom would continue another ten years, tripling the number of prison units by the turn of the century—110 prisons. Inmate population grew at almost the same pace, reaching 140,000 by the year 2000, one of the largest prison systems in the world.

While Rickie's situation was becoming more desperate, Keith Price's life had been improving. He had been warden at the Darrington Unit for about four years and he seemed to be one of the best wardens in the system, although there was no official recognition of that since he was still treated as a traitor by some of the old guard in TDCJ because he was enforcer of new ways to handle inmate problems. He had been named warden of two prison units that were in chaos. The speculation was that he was given very tough assignments by some who hoped he'd fail. Instead he turned them around, bringing order and respect among both staff and convict population.

His doctorate in behavioral science helped him see issues beyond society's 'lock them up' mentality. He said most inmates would be back in society in three years and any thoughts that they'd be better members of society was not based on fact. Most would not have gone through effective programs that brought a change in the problems and behavior that sent them to prison. His primary job as a warden was to keep criminals away from society for a time and keep them safe while they were there. He said prisons did that pretty well, and it took the lion share of money and energy. So they didn't do much to bring any changes in attitudes and behavior.

CHAPTER FIFTEEN

In mid-1989, Rickie and an inmate friend, Virgil Barfield, and another named Johnny Murray, made a plan to take over the Super Segregation cell block and kill a certain inmate. The target was from a Mexican Gang. Rickie heard the Mexican say he told the FBI that drugs and weapons were being smuggled into SuperSeg. He announced that loudly for all in the cell block to hear. The weapons were supposedly needed to kill him, which may be why he made such an announcement—hoping to stop it. Whether he was actually on a hit list before or not, that put him on one. Rickie put two and two together and concluded the snitch was the cause of Becky being arrested and sent to prison. Since her arrest, they were not allowed to communicate with each other to talk about details. Johnny also wanted the Mexican killed for some reason. Virgil just hated anyone who was a tattler, or 'snitch' in prison talk. Johnny was thrown out of AB for some connection with a homosexual, which was forbidden in AB rules. Gang members were ordered to attack him and one stabbed him. He had to be CareFlighted to a hospital and nearly died. When he recovered, he went on the attack stabbing AB members. After several such stabbings, he was sent to SuperSeg.

So the trio began putting their plan into action. Johnny made knives. They collected magazines, rolled them up, and stuck them together to make a pole. They attached a paper clip, bent into a hook, on the end.

There were always at least two officers in SuperSeg. But both of them have to escort an inmate to and from recreation and the shower. Virgil was in the cell next to the shower and the guard's table was in the hallway on the other side of the shower.

When the time came, Rickie went to recreation and then was locked in the shower, while the guards got the next inmate and escorted him to recreation. That left no one to watch the shower. Virgil passed the "pole" to Rickie so he could reach to the desk and hook the ring of keys on the desk about 6 feet away. He hooked the keys, but when he pulled them from the table, they were too heavy so the hook and one section of the "pole" came apart. Officers returned to find hook, magazine, and keys on the floor.

The warden and a team of officers quickly went through all the cells. They found the three knives. So that plan failed, but the trio was not about to give up.

Putting a Plan B in action took a few months. Rickie's competency trial took considerable time and attention. When it was over, Rickie went to work on the door to his cell. His goal was to cut the steel plate all the way around where it held the lock. Using whatever he could get that would cut steel, no matter how long and tedious the work was, he managed to cut three sides—top, bottom, and one side. It was getting close enough that he and his co-conspirators were getting excited in anticipation of getting the lock out so they could overpower the officers and take control of the cell block. With the keys, they could get in and kill the accused snitch. Then they would see how many inmates would join them to make a stand against the "army" that would come after them.

In Rickie's mind this would change the life—or existence—he was stuck in and hated. Either he would kill one or more of them and go to death row or they would kill him. He really had no preference between the two outcome scenarios.

But, alas, when he was so close, a team of officers came to do a routine shakedown and discovered the nearly severed steel plate. All that work and Plan B were for naught. Rickie was moved from that cell, number 12, next door into 11. He saw a large steel plate behind the toilet and was reminded of three years earlier when he was in cell 11. He had kicked the commode off the wall so the steel plate was put in when the toilet was replaced. He mostly remembered the pain when he kicked too high and nearly cut the heel off his foot on a ragged piece of metal.

One day, Rickie was sitting on his bunk—now a concrete slab instead of a metal cot that could be used for weapons. He was mulling possibilities for Plan C. The cell door opened, which never happened until after his hands had been cuffed behind him. A large man strolled in, stuck out a big hand, and introduced himself, "Hi, I'm Mike Barber."

Rickie recognized him from NFL Football. Barber played tight end for ten years, mostly with the Houston Oilers, then the Los Angeles Rams.

He was shocked not only that a famous NFL player was here, but even more that someone would walk, unannounced, into the cell of "the most violent man in Texas prison." But he sized up Barber with his big smile as a friendly guy. Besides, he looked big enough to defend himself.

Barber sat down on the concrete bunk next to Rickie. "How ya doing?"

"Okay," Rickie responded halfheartedly. "But how do you get to come into my cell?"

"The warden gave me permission. I'm glad you are good! But I came to tell you how you can do much better."

Rickie just sat quietly, still trying to figure out this scene. Barber went on to say that since retiring from football, he's dedicated his life to telling folks about the Lord, especially convicts in prisons and jails. Unlike most times when someone tried to talk to him about God, Rickie reacted calmly, listening for a few minutes before telling Barber that he was wasting his time. After the visitor left, Rickie sat a few minutes, wondering what just happened. He even went over some that Barber had said.

Suddenly, he jumped up thinking, *I don't need this junk!* He returned to figuring out a Plan C, to get the keys and take over SuperSeg. Virgil, one of the trio, was moved out of the SuperSeg cell block at Coffield, so now Plan C will just involve two men and Rickie had a great idea.

Johnny had the unusual skill of being able to slip out of handcuffs, so why not utilize that. Some officers were fascinated by how Johnny could slip his hands out, even when the cuffs were tight. Certain guards liked to entertain themselves by showing others what Johnny could do.

Rickie went to work making two large knives—almost swords. He first cut two strips off that steel plate behind the commode. They were about 18 inches long and 2 to 3 inches wide. Then he shaped and sharpened them, mostly on the concrete floor. That took well over a month, because officers were on alert and always made sure two are watching the cell block. Other inmates would give an alert when a guard came close. They also made noise to cover the cutting and sharpening. He used soap and water to try to help keep the work quieter.

In January 1990, the "swords" were finished and stashed inside his mattress, to be ready when the right time came. The 'right time' according to Plan C was when officers who liked to see Johnny do his trick with handcuffs were on duty. When they would put the cuffs on to take him to recreation, he would stop in front of cell 11 and show off with the handcuffs. The plan was when Johnny got his hands free, Rickie would slip the big knife into his hand so he could overpower the guards, get the keys, and let Rickie out carrying the other sword.

While waiting for the right guards and the right time, a new SuperSeg inmate was brought in and put in cell 12. His red hair and a fascination with his own feces got him the nickname "Dukey Red." He was constantly throwing human waste at officers. For some reason, he decided to pull out all the electric wiring in the cell. Guards came, beat him up, and moved him out of the cell block.

Maintenance people came and restored cell 12 so it could be used. One day when Rickie was gone to recreation and shower, officers moved what little property he had from number 11 back to cell 12. Rickie began complaining but to no avail. "At least give me my mattress!" he yelled.

"No, you have a brand-new one in number 12" was the reply. He argued and cussed for days, but it didn't help. He finally quit because he feared his begging would alert someone that there was something he wanted from 11. He kept hoping someone would be put in there so he could get him to pass the knives over to him, but it stayed empty until a mattress was needed somewhere else. An officer went into cell 11, picked up the mattress, and started down the cell block. He slung the mattress over his shoulder and two very large knives slid noisily to the concrete floor. That was the loud ending of Plan C.

Warden Alford and a squad of guards showed up quickly and naturally roughed up Rickie. Next day, sitting on the bunk looking at bruises, Rickie became very upset. The bruises were sore and especially hurt when he touched them, but he was used to that. What really upset him was the realization that everything he had tried to do for the last six months had failed. He spent the day going back and forth between frustration and anger. He refused a tray of food brought to him and ignored the normal yelling and cussing of other inmates.

The anger grew and overwhelmed the frustration. The most serious thing about the anger, this anger, was there seemed no way to fix it or even express it. Sure he could yell and cuss, but that was natural background noise in SuperSeg. Try as hard as he could, he could not come up with a way to channel the anger like he had always done. This anger was not directed at the despised officers or the prison system or gang enemies, as in the past. This anger and hatred was toward himself. While the last several years he had not won the war, he had won some battles, inflicting injury on many guards and inmates. He had enough of those "successes" to gain a form of "respect" in that he caused injury and damage to the extent that he must be handled in unique ways and avoided when possible.

Now, for months, he had failed in efforts to inflict injury and cause meaningful damage. Most of all he had not succeeded in the ultimate goal of actually killing someone. He hated his way of life and even more despised himself. All of a sudden, three plans in a row had failed.

My plans have nearly always worked, so what's wrong now? he thought. *Becky has gone to prison because of me. Three very good plans flopped, even with good helpers. What the dickens is going on?* He spent several days with his brain jumping between depression and pity and trying to devise a new plan to kill someone or be killed in the process. He even contemplated suicide, but then his anger kicked in and he declared, *I will NOT give them the satisfaction of carrying me out of here in a body bag!*

Maybe it's not WHAT is going on but WHO is against me. Could God be trying to protect that Mexican snitch, or these 'laws'? Or is He trying to stop me from making a last stand to kill or be killed? he pondered. He jumped up and kicked his shoes across the cell. *Where did that come from? Who is God and why would He give a hoot about me or anyone else in this prison?* Then his mind went to the time Captain Slider stood in front of his cell and said, "One of these days you will succeed in killing someone and get the death penalty but that's not the bad news, because then you will stand before your Creator to answer for all your sins."

He tried to ignore such thoughts but couldn't. He remembered Officer Robinson not being intimidated by his threats and treating him with some respect. What about Mike Barber coming in the cell, unafraid? Also, his mind recalled Jeff Nickell. They had met on the Eastham Unit during Rickie's first prison term. He made fun of Jeff because he claimed to be a Christian. He cussed him out whenever Jeff tried to talk to him about Jesus. When Jeff got out, he went with Calvary Commission, a Christian group that works with ex-cons. Several times in the last year, Jeff would come into SuperSeg and try to talk to Rickie about the Lord. When Rickie wouldn't listen, Jeff would sit cross-legged in front of the cell and sing Gospel songs and talk about Jesus. Rickie generally ignored him, but now his mind was replaying those songs and the things he had refused to listen to.

Rickie's brain was in chaos. It jumped around like a crazy person. One minute cussing the #&*@# prison system, then hating himself because of where his life had gotten him, interrupted by the sweet voice of Jeff singing, "Jesus loves me," then an officer drawing a finger across his throat and pointing to Rickie, to Carl Robinson quoting a verse about God's Grace, and back to trying to find a plan to get out to kill the Mexican and some guards.

That turmoil continued for days. When Rickie finally collapsed in fatigue, he slept three or four hours and woke up angry and filled with hate and rage. Then his brain would go back through all the competing images and sounds again and again. Even when he could sleep a little bit, dreams kept the turmoil churning in his head.

Finally, Rickie made himself get control of his thoughts. He decided to make an effort to consciously analyze all these competing messages. A central theme emerged that God was behind his failures. So, *Why would God have any thought about me? I have cussed Him, I have made fun of His Bible, told many people that it's a worthless book, written by men who want to control you. I have done everything that preachers and others say will send you to hell. Obviously, He is not interested in me, so apparently He's protecting these other people, my enemies.*

So much thinking about God surprised Rickie. He thought back to Chocolate Bayou Baptist Church. He remembered his mother and others talking about the Lord. So he didn't doubt that there is a God. But he's sure God is not interested in Him. He would not answer his prayers to make his mom and dad a happy couple. And He has apparently not been interested in Rickie's life from school up through drugs, crimes, fights, and prison. *So if He's working against me now, it has to be because of my enemies.*

The rational moments didn't last too long. They were overtaken with some inmate complaining at the top of his lungs or by officers requiring him to undress and turn around, then put clothes on and get his hands cuffed behind his back to go to recreation and shower. The prison routines always brought the anger and hatred to the forefront. But more and more that hatred turned inward on himself.

This vicious cycle went on for days. Then Rickie realized that what had impressed him was the peace that Jeff and Carl Robinson had even when being rejected or cussed out and the confidence Mike Barber showed coming in uninvited. *I wish I could be like that*, he thought. But immediately came, *There's no way, buddy. They're different, they're not like you. You have to be tough to survive and you need to teach those "goon squads" and others to respect you.*

He got out that Bible Tony Rice had thrown away and started flipping pages and looking for something that made sense. Most of what he read did not make sense. He remembered the first letter that Bob Norris of Hospitality House had sent him. He had stuck that one in with some mail from his Mother and Becky. All the others he tore up as he made fun of them. But now he remembered that Bob had said some things like Jeff and Carl, so he dug it out and read it. Norris had quoted some scripture verses and he found them in the Bible. He got down on the floor of his cell and said, "God, what's going on? I can't handle this. I need you to fix things. Amen."

Suddenly, a warning flashed through his mind, *What do you think you are doing? Talking to cement? What good will that do? And while you are down there, anyone walking by can see you being stupid!!*

He got up and looked around—he didn't see anyone near his cell door. But soon the flood of conflicting messages returned and the conclusion that God was behind his problems came back. He got a sheet and hung it up to cover the door of his cell so no one could see in. Then he knelt down and again asked God to explain what's going on and what he needed to do. Nothing.

And the warnings returned, *You fool. Remember all the things you have said about God? What about the way you have made fun of him in front of lots of people? And now, you expect him to come and take care of you? You are crazy, aren't you?*

That jumping back and forth between begging God and hearing in his mind how ridiculous that was went on back and forth for maybe two more days. Rickie was exhausted as well as confused, angry, upset, ready to die, and wanting answers. About one midnight, he shook his head violently, like trying to get rid of all the thoughts. Again, he read through the letter from Norris and thumbed through the Bible to find the verses Norris used.

One verse stood out that night. He read it over and over and looked at the verses before it and after it. He looked at other passages, but kept coming back to Matthew 11:28, "**Come to me, all you who are weary and burdened, and I will give you rest**."

Rickie's brain lit up, "Rest! Rest! That's what I need, **rest**!" He read the verses before and after it, ²⁷"All things have been committed to me by my Father. No one knows the Son except the Father, and no one knows the Father except the Son and those to <u>whom the Son chooses</u> to reveal him.

²⁸ "Come to me, all you who are weary and burdened, and I will give you rest.
  ²⁹ Take my yoke upon you and learn from me, for I am gentle and humble in heart, and you will find <u>rest for your souls</u>."

Without even thinking, Rickie flopped face down on the concrete floor and said out loud, "Jesus, I am weary and burdened. I am coming to you as you said. Please, **please**, give me rest! Like you said, I'm choosing you and I ask you to choose me. I accept your yoke and I need rest for my soul." Then he just lay there several moments. His body felt limp. He got up on his hands and knees then stood. He felt light. His mind and body both felt different. He sat down on the cement bunk then leaned over, drew his feet up, and immediately he was sound asleep.

T R (Red) and Celestia (Torchie) Smith

Celestia holding new baby Rickie

Rickie had a normal middle-class childhood

Becoming adult was not as normal

Rickie Smith in prison clothes

Celestia was Rickie's most frequent and regular visitor

Warden Keith Price

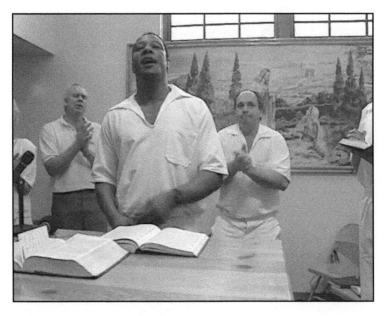

Rickie loves music

CHAPTER SIXTEEN

At 8:00 AM, February 2, 1990, Rickie Smith was awakened by an officer bringing breakfast to his cell. He slowly got up and took the tray being offered through the "bean slot" in the door. He set the tray on his bed and sat back down. He realized that he felt rested. He thought about five hours earlier when he had surrendered himself to the Lord and felt the tension and anger drain away. He assumed the peace he felt at 2:00 AM would be gone this morning and he would return to the chaos of recent days. But the peace was still there and the angry thoughts that usually greeted him each morning had not showed up. He was not only surprised but truly amazed at the difference in how he felt.

He finished his coffee and some of the breakfast and pushed the tray aside, "I've got to write a letter to Bob Norris." He dug out some paper and a pencil and wrote, telling Bob he was the first person he had told that "I gave my life to Jesus. Thank you for helping me to find my way."

Yes, everything in the Super Segregation cell block of the Coffield Unit of the Texas Department of Corrections looked and sounded different to Rickie that morning. There was still all kinds of cussing and yelling bouncing off the concrete walls, the loud sounds of door locks and door slams and officers still pacing up and down in front of the 12 cells, looking for whatever was happening—but to Rickie it's completely different from yesterday.

He had to tell someone, so he got to the dayroom when Johnny

Murray, his most recent partner in crime, was there. He wanted to see his face, "Johnny, I want you to know what I did. Last night, I called on the Lord, Jesus, and He gave me peace."

Johnny threw a fit, "What are you talking about, man? That's just crazy! You know that all that is ..." and he launched into a profanity-laced tirade about God and aimed at Rickie and anyone else who could be fooled like that. The veins in his neck stood out, he had a really crazy look on his face. The amazing thing was that Rickie just looked at him and let him explode and when he finished, simply said, "I used to think that way, Johnny, but now I know the truth."

In SuperSeg, when Rickie talked about Jesus inmates joined in, some on one side a few on the other. Rickie didn't want to argue so he would move back in his cell, pick up the Bible, and try to ignore the racket—until someone yelled, "I bet the warden will be happy!"

That brought a flood of anger into Rickie's mind. He thought of how much he hated that Warden. Then came reminders of some particular officers and that grew into his whole war with the prison system. Finally, it jumped to those gang enemies just a few cells away and especially that "snitch" he needed to kill because he got Becky into jail.

The familiar frustration and rage was interrupted by a sudden memory of the peace he felt when he got up this morning. He flopped face down on the concrete floor and said, "Oh God, what can I do? I know you accepted me. I know something's different. But I'm stuck in here with all these people who will kill me if they have a chance and under the thumbs of guards and the warden I hate. What can I do?"

Again he felt a peace, so he ignored the noise in the cell block and opened the Bible and read several pages. He didn't find the answer to "what can I do?" but he felt confirmation that God is real and He cares.

In SuperSeg there were frequent interruptions, meals brought in, trips out for recreation and shower, guards checking cells and the constant noise of eleven other inmates complaining, accusing, joking, cussing.

Occasionally, something triggered the anger, which has been the primary force of his life for several years. He would again get on the floor and pray, "God, you promised peace and rest and I felt your peace, but now the hatred is back. Help me!" Most of his praying was done on the floor, because he felt so unworthy to even talk to God, much less to stand in His presence.

That pattern occurred several times over a few days. But more and more Rickie realized he was different inside. When Officer Carl Robinson came on duty, Rickie was excited to tell him what he had done. They chatted and Robinson assured Rickie he was on track, but that he had to learn new ways of thinking and a new way of living. He also pointed out that God is aware of that process and does not expect perfection.

He spent a lot of time reading the Bible. It was difficult for him with his sixth grade education and mild dyslexia. But instead of giving up and chunking it aside, like he had so many times, he kept after it. He got a dictionary to help with words. He was surprised at himself and his patience. More and more he could concentrate and ignore the chaos of the cell block. He also cleaned out his cell. He got rid of girly magazines, books, and anything else that could draw his attention away from his new "friend," Jesus. It was obvious he had so much to learn, but rather than being discouraged, he was eager to soak up as much possible.

One of the things he got rid of was a radio. Captain Slider had promised to help Rickie and he was able to get his personal property back into his cell and restored the privilege of going to the commissary. That happened shortly before Rickie called out to the Lord. But he now considered the radio one of the distractions and an inmate named Rudy got it. Soon Rickie talked and shared scripture with another SuperSeg inmate, who then prayed and accepted Jesus, too. What's amazing was this was a gang member of the Mexican Mafia, a prime enemy. When the new convert said he would like to have a radio to listen to gospel music and preaching, Rickie asked Rudy to give it to him. Rudy said, "OK, if you'll give me $20 of commissary funds."

Unlike previous extortion efforts, this time Rickie sent the commissary money to Rudy, who then said, "Hey Christian, pray about it. You're Jack." He kept the radio and the money. Rickie became very angry and started gathering the materials to make a "zip gun" to use on Rudy when he had to come by on the way to the shower.

Suddenly, he was reminded in his spirit of the peace he had gained and his commitment to Christ. Then a scripture verse he had heard came to mind as he remembered it, "The Lord wouldn't put no more on me than I can handle and He'll provide a way of escape." He got on his knees, "Lord, I don't know why you're allowing this to happen. I want that radio so this new Christian can listen to Gospel music and preaching. I don't know why you're letting this happen, but please, show me."

In his spirit, Rickie heard, *I want you to learn to walk in forgiveness and not your old ways. I'm dealing with your pride.*

That was a strange line of thought to Rickie. His reaction was, *Pride? What can I be proud of? I've made a complete mess of my life, hurt my parents and so many others, I'm stuck in the worst place in the whole world and called the most violent man in prison. I am really ashamed, not proud.*

Then the Lord helped him see that it was his pride that got him where he was, *I never let anybody take anything from me,* he realized. *If somebody looked at me the wrong way, we fought. I always had to be top dog. I sought, even demanded respect, but the only respect I got was from fear.*

Oh God, forgive my pride. Thanks for making me see it. *Now, Lord, help me overcome it and deal the right way with these problems that keep coming up.* Then he got up, sat down, and wrote a letter to Rudy. He explained, "There's not enough radios in this whole prison, or enough money in the whole world to pay for what I have now, the peace that I have." Then, he told Rudy what he has learned about living with Jesus. Every time Rudy was escorted by Rickie's cell, he had a 'tough guy' look on his face. Rickie spoke each time he saw him, but Rudy would look away.

Several months later, Rudy had apparently hit bottom and sent a note down the cell block to Rickie. It said, "I need Jesus. Tell me how you found Him and the peace you have. Please forgive me for stealing the radio. I am trying to figure out the best way to kill myself."

Rickie responded that he knew what he's going through, "What it's like to be without hope. I wanted to die. I was without hope, too." Then he explained the Gospel and how to pray. Rudy said he turned his life over to Christ. They had many conversations about God and the Bible until a few months later when Rudy was moved out of the SuperSeg cell block. A few years later, Rickie was told that Rudy was still actively serving the Lord.

There were other Aryan Brotherhood gang members in SuperSeg and they could hear Rickie talking about becoming a Christian, so he specifically informed them that he can no longer be a part of the gang. He also invited them to accept the Lord. Their reactions were bitter and ugly which really confirmed the hatred they had for Jesus and many people. Rickie explained that he was different now and cannot be part of such a hateful, mean, outlaw group, period.

Rickie and the new Christian became good friends and prayer partners. After Rudy sent the radio to him, he would turn it up for Rickie to hear when there was preaching on Dallas station KCBI. Later, when he was transferred from SuperSeg to another unit, they continued to write, pray, and help each other.

Bob Norris immediately responded to the letter Rickie sent him the day after his prayer of turning to God. Norris expressed elation for the decision and promised to help in any way and to pray for him. Norris was added to his visitor list and eventually could come to meet Rickie, visit, and to help with Bible study.

A car salesman in Dallas, Jack Wilcox, attended a weekly Bible Study Breakfast with other men at Prestonwood Baptist Church. He learned about prison ministry opportunities and was drawn to that. He got qualified as a volunteer chaplain within Texas prisons. He began coming to Coffield Unit, one of the closest to Dallas, on weekends. He enjoyed ministering with the inmates so much that he would drive his van to the prison, spend Saturday talking to them, sleep in his van, and spend Sunday in the prison also. He was permitted to go into the Super

Segregation cell block. He would go to each cell to chat with the convict and offer to pray with them and to help them with Bible studies.

Rickie opened up to Wilcox and they became good friends. He told of the recurring bouts of anger which interfered with the peace he felt from the Lord. As they discussed it, Wilcox affirmed that God had forgiven Rickie's rebellion, but explained that Rickie had to forgive all those who have harmed him.

"Oh man! I don't think I can do that," was the reaction. Wilcox used various scripture verses to try to help Rickie understand God's Word. He used the familiar verses commonly called "The Lord's Prayer" in Matthew, chapter 6. He had Rickie read the passage then said, "In verse 12, Jesus says, 'Forgive us our debts, as we also have forgiven our debtors,' then in verses 14 and 15, 'For if you forgive men when they sin against you, your heavenly Father will also forgive you. But if you do not forgive men their sins, your Father will not forgive your sins.' That's pretty plain, isn't it?" Rickie was startled.

Wilcox explained, "Yes, God has accepted you, as Jesus promised, but you now have to learn to do things God's way. His way is to forgive your sins against Him, and He has done that. But His way also includes expecting you to be forgiving toward those who have wronged you. Unforgiveness goes with hatred and bitterness and that's why those ugly feelings keep showing up. They are tools Satan can use to try to set you back."

All that week, Rickie pondered that and read scriptures over and over and thought of some of the people he had despised over these years of gang and prison wars. When Wilcox came the next weekend, he asked how he was doing with forgiveness. Rickie said he understood the principle and believed that's what God required, and he's ready to work on it but, "I can tell you this: it ain't going to be easy." They prayed about it. When Wilcox left, Rickie began a list of those he needed to forgive.

Every week, Wilcox would come and see how he could help. It was a big relief to Rickie to learn that personal forgiveness was not required for anyone who was no longer available for Rickie to talk to. But he must forgive them in his own heart to get rid of the hatred. And those he could talk to he could tell personally. But every time he came, Wilcox would remind Rickie of the importance of letting go of the hurts and bitterness that had built up over so many very tough years.

Rickie began his project with some guards in the cell block who physically or verbally were hard on him. Right off the bat, he learned that while he was trying to forgive a guy, he often needed to apologize to him for his own behavior as well. Some were willing to listen and respond favorably, others not so much. He told Wilcox about a guard who frequently twisted handcuffs and other painful things, but when Rickie apologized and said he forgave him, the guard sneered and walked away. Wilcox explained that's OK, "God is dealing with you, not the others. He wants to shape you into the image of His Son, Jesus—who even asked forgiveness for those who crucified Him."

Each time he apologized or forgave someone, he felt a little lighter, a little cleaner, and was spurred on to learn more about how to live God's way in one of the most difficult places to live.

Conversations between inmates a few cells apart were loud enough for most others to hear. A new resident was brought in and put next to Rickie. He was a black man and a homosexual, two things Rickie despised. One day Rickie was at the door of his cell having a Christian chat with another guy a few cells away. The new guy didn't want to hear about Jesus. Suddenly, he reached through the bars of his cell and threw a cup of urine into Rickie's cell. It was a direct hit, in the face and all over him.

Rickie sent messages down the block, gathered the parts he needed, and made a 'zip gun' to shoot the neighbor as soon as he had the chance. (A zip gun is made with whatever can be a barrel, a handle, and a rubber band, or something to move a "firing pin." Projectiles can be improvised darts or even bullets. Some zip guns are as dangerous to the shooter as to the target.) It seems that God delayed the chance to use it long enough to get Rickie's attention. In his spirit he realized that shooting the guy would take away the peace he has enjoyed so much. Back down on the floor, he asked God to forgive him and show him "how to deal with this guy—black and homosexual." He tore up the zip gun and flushed the pieces down the toilet. Then he explained to the neighbor that he was a Christian and although he wanted to hurt him, he couldn't do that as a Christian. He also said, "If I have done things to disturb you, please forgive me. A few months ago, I didn't want to hear about Jesus either, so I understand. But I also ask you to let me talk with my Christian friends." Apparently the apology was accepted and they didn't have any more trouble.

Rickie wrote to Bob Norris regularly. In a letter after the urine incident, he expressed some feelings he had, "I really don't want to go to heaven with blacks, homosexuals, and child molesters. I don't want them to be my brothers."

Norris responded, "Wait a minute! What about you? Who are you to determine who God forgives? If those people have called on Christ, they're no more a child molester than you are what you used to be." He said, "They are Christians, they are forgiven. Who are you to determine who gets forgiven and who doesn't? You need to just be thankful that you have been forgiven."

That set off a string of emotions, causing Rickie to look more deeply at himself than before. He was confronted with his views of white supremacy and realized the color of his skin wasn't going to mean anything on judgment day, thinking, *It's the blood of Jesus Christ that transcends all our culture, all our race, our education. It covers someone like me, who would not amount to anything in this world.* That began a long process of overcoming racial and other prejudices that had built up since his dad told him not to bring any more black friends home.

After her release from prison, Becky resumed involvement with ex-cons. Ricky wrote her a letter explaining that he had accepted Jesus, become a Christian, and was a changed man. He would no longer be involved in drugs and other previous activity.

That didn't sit well with her, "You got me involved in all this and now you want to be a Christian?" she wrote.

Soon, Jeff Lykens was released from prison and Becky picked him up at the Walls Unit in Huntsville. They hit it off and began a relationship. She told Rickie she wanted to marry Jeff. He responded, in effect, if that's what they want, "Fine." Lykens was the inmate who tried twice to kill Rickie on New Year's Eve before they reconciled.

Before long, Rickie got word, through a complicated network involving a prison guard, that an ex-con gang member wanted Rickie's approval to set the house on fire and then shoot Becky and Jeff if they ran out. That ex-con had several reasons to target Becky and Jeff. For one thing, their relationship and betraying Rickie was against gang rules. Another was that he claimed it was Becky's fault the laws discovered the plan to ambush the prison caravan carrying Rickie to one of his trials as it crossed the Trinity River bridge. He said Becky was supposed to be one of the drivers and she got scared at the last minute. Rickie responded through the officer bringing the information that he was now a Christian and certainly did not want anything like that to happen.

Sometime later, an investigator for the prison system came to Rickie asking him to tell about a murder they accuse Jeff of doing in prison. They tried to use Jeff's taking Becky as leverage to get Rickie to get revenge on Jeff. He refused, "I am a Christian and I belong to Jesus. My past is washed in His blood. I will not put my possibility of witnessing to former friends in jeopardy."

Rickie was well aware that attitudes don't change easily. A few inmates and some officers recognized the difference in talk and action in his life, but the vast majority, like the warden, paid no attention. His reputation far outweighed any new information. Many assumed it was an attempt to con his way out of SuperSeg, or a scheme to get the drop on some target.

Rickie understood that, *I've earned my reputation, was even proud of it*, he thought. *I've conned and manipulated goons for years*. Then he prayed, "Lord, help me to be true to your ways and give me patience with all those around me."

CHAPTER SEVENTEEN

In 1990, on Groundhog Day, Rickie Smith took on a new label, "Christian." Of course, to everyone else he was still known as "most violent man in Texas prison."

In 1990, the Texas Prison System also had a new label. The name had changed to Texas Department of Criminal Justice (TDCJ). It's an umbrella title that incorporated other aspects of dealing with those convicted of crimes. The Pardons and Paroles Division oversaw reintegration of convicts in society when released from incarceration. The Community Justice Assistance Division dealt with felons for punishment, supervision, and rehab within the community. The largest part of TDCJ was the Institutional Division which operated the prisons for adult offenders. Juvenile offenders were handled in a separate agency. It took a long time for many people to add that "J" to TDC and only in official language were prisons referred to as the "Institutional Division."

In 1990, the Texas Department of Criminal Justice, Institutional Division, housed 48,000 inmates. That's almost three times as many as when Rickie Smith came in. (Prison population tripled again in the next fifteen years.) Ten new prison units were opened in 1989 and 1990 and the building accelerated, adding seventy-six prisons by 1998. In 2004, Texas' prison population, 150,000, made it the largest state system and the third largest in the whole world.

In 1990, Federal District Judge William Wayne Justice ended the monitoring of prisons by the special master he created nine years earlier.

However, he still had the prison system under his supervision. The special master's office in Houston was closed and attorneys representing inmates assumed the role of watching TDCJ's progress in complying with the court's directives. Judge Justice said the change "represents a significant step toward the conclusion of this litigation." However his oversight of Texas prisons would continue twelve more years.

Also by 1990, the Texas legislature had stepped up its interest and appropriated over a billion dollars for construction of all those prison units, and greatly increased budgets for more staff, more training, and improved operation.

A side note to 1990—David Ruiz was in a Super Segregation cell down the row from Rickie Smith. Ruiz started the federal court take-over of Texas prisons and the resulting chaos nearly twenty years before with his handwritten lawsuit claiming brutality and inhumane treatment. When the yearlong federal trial concluded in late 1979, Ruiz was moved to a federal prison for his own protection. Two years later he was finally granted parole. A couple of years later he was jailed four months for violating parole. Then, in 1985 he received a life sentence for aggravated robbery in Austin and again was put in federal custody. He filed, and won, a court case to be returned to Texas where he was put into administrative segregation, including time in SuperSeg. He had already spent much more of his life in prison than out.

Again—in 1990, Keith Price was gaining a reputation as a very effective warden. He was sent into the turmoil of the Darrington Unit, becoming the fifth warden in two years. Within a couple of years, Darrington was operating as smoothly as any prison, even though it housed many of the toughest, hardened men in the whole system. Price used a combination of strict rules and fair treatment to gain the respect of most inmates as well as the prison staff. His early experience in the old ways of handling troublemakers, his commitment to the new (and constitutional) ways, and his education in behavioral science combined well with his personality for him to oversee the transformation of one of the worst prisons. This was the second assignment, as a beginning warden, to a very challenging situation, and the second successful outcome.

Finally in 1990, while the majority of Texas Department of Criminal Justice employees were trained in the new ways of dealing with inmate issues—or have adapted to the new ways—there were still holdouts. They generally did their jobs within guidelines enough to keep from being fired, but their preference was still the old "tough boss man" approach. That seemed to be especially seen in the attitudes of some senior officers and administrative personnel who have been with the system ten years or more. The conflicting operation philosophies were more evident in verbal confrontations and complaints than in action, because the guidelines of the federal court were how the TDCJ administration viewed prison operation.

In December 1990, the *Houston Chronicle* published an extensive review and analysis of the status of Texas Prisons after ten years of reform and turmoil. It showed opinions deeply divided among staff at all levels and even among inmates over the value of the changes brought about by the federal court. The *Dallas Morning News* and other newspapers also weighed in on prison operations and the state's governance of the criminal justice system.

One of the most outspoken employee critics of the changes was Lon Bennett Glenn. Among his prime targets was Keith Price. Glenn worked thirty years beginning as an officer and finished as a warden. When he retired as an assistant warden, he wrote a book, published in 2001. Called *The Largest Hotel Chain in Texas*, it equated putting criminals in prisons operated as dictated by Federal Judge William Wayne Justice and inmates lawyers with sending them to hotels. He apparently expressed the feelings of a number of employees and former employees of TDCJ.

Price was singled out in the book as having been a gung-ho officer and leader in the old ways of prisoner treatment who then turned on his peers. In the job as head of the new office of Operational Audits, Price investigated complaints against staff. The results sometimes brought demotions and even dismissals at all levels. Glenn referred to the riot at the Eastham Unit where Price led the charge against rebellious inmates without noting that Price argued against the charge but finally followed a direct order from the warden. He saw Price's appointment to Operational Audits as a betrayal. Glenn wrote of Price, "As a result of his eat-your-own-kind persona, most TDC employees viewed him as somewhat of a Judas."

He quoted Price as saying, "Our organization evolved and I simply changed with it, which seems to me to be the only thing a thinking man would do."

Glenn summarized, "When the day comes that I become so 'pragmatic' that I sacrifice my own fellow employees in order to worship at the altar of the likes of William Wayne Justice, I would prefer being a member of an extinct species." In chapter eight of "The Largest Hotel Chain in Texas" along with stories of gang murders and efforts to remove weapons and other prohibited contraband, he tells of what he called "The Best-Kept Secret in Texas." Recall that the issues of 'building tenders' had smoldered in the federal court case with TDC denying that inmates were used in controlling other inmates. Glenn refers to a book written by a prison staff attorney, Steve Martin, who related going to Texas Attorney General Mark White saying, "General, the TDC has a sophisticated building-tender system under which serious abuses occur frequently, maybe daily."

"You mean," asked White, "we're using inmates as guards?"

"You are," replied Martin, "probably since the first day the lawsuit was filed."

"You mean they've been lying to me all these years?"

Glenn's conclusion was this demonstrates the state government was out of touch with prison reality, "Given the well-documented figures showing an unworkable staff-to-inmate ratio, who did they think was running the state's prison system?" His book defends the pre-court ordered operations, including building tenders, as preferable to the new ways.

In the same chapter, he claimed that because of Martin's disclosure to the attorney general, "The only person more reviled by rank-and-file TDC employees than attorney Steve Martin was the ex-security captain

166

from the Eastham Unit, Keith Price, who had been appointed as the head of the new TDC Operational-Audits office." Later, Glenn says he declined a potential promotion because of concern that it might put him on the Darrington Unit staff under Warden Price. Nowhere in his book does Glenn acknowledge that Price had made a difference in the operation of the Darrington Unit. Naturally, Glenn was just one of many expressing their opinions and feelings both ways.

Darrington was one of the older prison units, created in 1917, along with the Eastham Unit. They were added to the ten already operating. It's named for John Darrington who came from Alabama as a plantation owner in 1841. When it was turned into a prison, it was still called Darrington Plantation and emphasis was on agricultural production using inmate labor in the tough conditions of that era. It became known as Darrington State Farm until it was closed during World War II. The prison reopened in 1946 and still today the primary activity is farming. A lot of the work is done by inmates using hoes and other hand tools.

Darrington was still struggling with adapting to the new federal mandated guidelines when Keith Price took over as warden. His success in turning things around came from a combination of teaching and enforcing the new ways of operation for staff and separating the most difficult inmates and firmly cracking down on those who violated rules. The problem convicts were segregated into special cell blocks. There they had freedom to yell and cuss and destroy their own cell contents, but they were only being heard by each other and not by the general population inmates. And they did not have much physical access to attack each other, a lot like SuperSeg.

In other cell blocks, officers were trained to recognize potential problems and report them. Special squads of officers would come to deal with suspected violations, control inmates and search for prohibited items. These were like the old SORT but without the mistreatment and violence.

Price and the chaplains created more opportunities for families to visit. Security is the first concern of prison, so inmates had to follow the rules to qualify for the additional freedom in family visits. That was incentive for better behavior and the additional time with loved ones helped improve attitudes.

That's one example of Price's desire to blend concern for rules and more respectful treatment of human beings. In an interview in 1990, the warden talked about the dilemma facing those operating prisons, "One of the problems I think our society has decided to do, which I feel is a mistake, is that they feel the answer to crime and criminals is to use prison as a form of exile. They forget that inmates are still members of society, and the numbers show that they're gonna be a member of society again in a very short period of time—around three years on average. And the idea that inmates are going to be better adapted when they come out is really not based in fact."

He recognized that prisons are very difficult places for people whether they are behind the bars or in front, "People that wind up in prison, inmates, generally are society's rejects. They've been unable to do the things other people do to make life a success, whether it's because of an abusive parent, addiction to some substance, stupidity, being unable to read or write, they've been failures and have chosen alternate means—that is, crime. But they haven't been successful at that—because they got caught."

On the other hand, Price saw challenges for the officers, too, "The correctional officer has to deal with people so maladjusted that society says they can't live amongst them anymore. It's conflict day after day, hour after hour and it really takes a toll, from broken marriages to financial problems to substance abuse—it's continual."

He talked from personal experience about the pressures as they helped end his first marriage and brought emotional strain that almost forced him out of the career. Now, he has a different perspective, "A warden gets to influence a lot of people. There's a lot of inmates, a lot of staff that all work for me. Hopefully, the kind of example that I can set will maybe make a difference in somebody's life. For whatever reason, God has chosen me to be where I am now. And I just try to do the best I can to live up to what it is that God wants me to do."

While Keith Price was trying to live up to what God wanted him to do as warden at Darrington, Rickie was devouring scripture to learn what he should do as a Christian. It was clear to him that he should be baptized. He knew that being baptized at Chocolate Bayou Baptist Church didn't mean anything—he was just trying to make his mother happy. He told officers in SuperSeg that he wanted to be baptized. It was a novel request to them, but they passed the word to the Coffield Chaplain, Jerry Grooms, who came to talk with him. When he determined Rickie was sincere, he made a request with the warden who immediately said, "Absolutely not!"

Rickie pleaded with Grooms who made a second request and talked with the warden. It was denied again. But Rickie had his heart set on "following his Lord" in baptism. Grooms took the third request to the chief of chaplains, Emmett Solomon, who went to the warden and convinced him this was an important spiritual event and should be honored by the prison system.

Warden Jimmy Alford finally gave in. "I'm putting enough chains, locks, cuffs and leg shackles on him that if you let go of him, he'll drown." Rickie wanted Bob Norris to baptize him and Bob agreed.

When the day arrived, the team came to take him to the chapel to be baptized. They went through the usual routine of handcuffing behind his back, then opened the door to attach leg shackles and a belly chain. The procession proceeded through several hallways and into the chapel. Chaplain Grooms and Bob Norris had to help him struggle into the baptistery with the heavy chains and no hands. He had a bit of disappointment coming in because the chapel was empty and he knew the Bible says to be baptized as a witness to salvation. But when Norris lifted him to his feet from being immersed, Rickie felt nothing but pure joy. As the procession made its way back to SuperSeg, Rickie's clothes and the chains were dripping wet, leaving a trail. It was shift change, so he realized there were about twice as many officers in the halls to be 'witnesses' of the huge smile and to see the tears of joy on his face. He announced, "**I have chains on my body but there are none on my heart!** *Real* **freedom in the middle of** *real* **prison!!**"

One weekend, Chaplain Wilcox did not show up at Coffield. Rickie assumed he had business or illness. The next week, Rickie mentioned that he missed their visit last Saturday. Wilcox explained that he attended a chaplain's convention in Austin.

"How was it?" Rickie asked.

"It was very good," Wilcox responded. "A good time of sharing and getting updated with each other. Oh, and the highlight was the testimony of a Christian Warden."

"Really," was the skeptical reply. "Who was that?"

"Warden Keith Price of Darrington Unit."

"No way!" Rickie exploded. "He certainly wasn't a Christian when I met him." Then he told about a time he attacked another inmate but got grabbed by an officer who took him to the captain's office—Captain Keith Price. There was talk of having a discipline hearing but even though there were several officers in the room, Rickie lunged at one with a knife. Captain Price threw him to the floor and subdued him under the desk, using hands and feet apparently breaking Rickie's nose. (That's the inmate's recollection. Price claims no memory of such an event.)

Wilcox wasn't startled, as he had heard so many stories involving the inmate. He commented, "Well, it sounds like you need to add Warden Price to your forgiveness list." Rickie brushed it off. Every Saturday they would chat, study the Bible, and pray. And usually, Wilcox would ask how the forgiveness list was going and Rickie would tell him about letters he had sent and responses he had gotten. They acknowledged that Rickie's task was to deal with those he saw or could contact and not be concerned about anyone who was not available. Also, Wilcox said, "You are not responsible for those who reject your effort, only for obeying God yourself."

After a few weeks, the chaplain asked whether Rickie had written to Warden Price about forgiveness. The answer: "No, I can't do it." After they had spent a few months on the forgiveness list and several scripture lessons on it, Wilcox had reached a point of frustration. When he asked this time about Price, Rickie said, "No, I've tried several times but I can't make it sound real, so I tore 'em up."

The chaplain exploded, "Then put him on it," Wilcox yelled. "You cannot get closer to God as long as you hold onto anger and unforgiveness at Price and the whole system." He turned and walked away, leaving Rickie standing at his cell door.

It was probably a good thing that door was locked. Rickie's anger boiled up, "Who does he think he is?" he fumed as he watched Wilcox being let out of the cell block. "He's not in here! They never jump on him in handcuffs, body-slam him. He comes every weekend and then goes back to Dallas." He sat down on the bunk with his face in his hands, "I can't do it. Not him."

That evening, Rickie replayed everything Wilcox had said, and he prayed for God's help. Suddenly, he said, "Oh God, forgive me! I've been fighting against you. I realize that now. Please, help me."

He got up, dug out his tablet and a pencil, and started writing a letter to Warden Price. It just flowed out, three pages long. He gave a short version of how Tony Rice threw a Bible out of his cell and Officer Robinson put it in Rickie's cell. He told how he eventually 'accepted Christ as his savior.' Then he asked Price to forgive him for all the trouble he had caused him.

A couple of weeks later, Rickie got a letter from Price. He said, "I am very happy to hear that you became a Christian." He also cautioned, "Time will tell if you are being truthful with me. If so, TDCJ will have no more trouble out of you, because you cannot receive Christ without a change in behavior." Rickie read the letter over and over and pondered the last sentence. He also felt good inside. He was glad he had finally taken that big step Jack Wilcox had harped on for months.

A few weeks later, a letter came from Sammy Buenatello, in the TDCJ Classification Office, saying he is coming to see Rickie and review his record. After that meeting, Rickie was taken to a state classification hearing. In that hearing, Buenatello said, "Warden Price is going to give you a chance. He is putting his testicles on the chopping block and you better not cross him." That started a few months of bureacratic red tape aimed at getting him off Super Segregation and moved to the Darrington Unit.

Finally, Rickie wrote to his dad, Red Smith. There had been almost no contact for several years. He told of his choice and how Jesus has changed him. Red responded and they began writing back and forth. Of course, in his zeal, Rickie wanted to convince his dad to become a Christian. He quoted scriptures and explained what Jesus has done for us. Red was so pleased that his son had changed from the monster he had become, but he was disturbed by all the talk in the letters and in the Bible about blood.

In one letter he even referred to the appearance of becoming cannibals, particularly in John, chapter 6. John 6:53–56: So Jesus said to them, "I assure you: Unless you eat the flesh of the Son of Man and drink His blood, you do not have life in yourselves." He, obviously was speaking 'Spiritually.'

Of course, many of Jesus' followers had the same problem as Red with those statements and went away from following him. Rickie wrote how Jesus, in the following verses, explained to his disciples that he was speaking spiritually and not of literal physical blood and flesh. Rickie went through a Bible and filled in many personal notes related to God's requirement for sacrifices in atonement for sin. He sent that Bible to his dad, who apparently read it all. Then he came to visit for the first time since Rickie was in prison.

That visit, as were all with inmates in high security, was where Red sat in front of a steel cage, looking through bulletproof glass and talking on a phone to each other. They handily "cleared the air" between them and moved on to father-son chatting. Rickie explained how excited he was with his new life and expressed the hope that Red would join him in following Christ. Red said he would like that. Rickie explained the process of confessing sins and repenting and asking God's forgiveness and asking Jesus to put His Spirit in him—like taking on Jesus' flesh and blood.

Red agreed and both men knelt on the floor with the steel wall between them, and barely able to hear each other. Also, it was a struggle for Rickie because even though he was in the small cage, he still had to wear leg chains attached to a belt. But there they prayed together and Red followed the lead of his adopted son to acknowledge he was a sinner and accepted Christ into his life. That was such a joy to Rickie and to Red. He was retired from his construction career, living alone in a small house on a finger of a lake at the edge of Grandbury, Texas. He was not in good health, as his hard living seemed to have caught up with him.

A lady was in the visiting room that day as a volunteer chaplain. She saw the Smiths on their knees in prayer and she joined them. They got acquainted and she wrote to Rickie that she would pick up Red and bring him to prison for visits.

Inmate Tony Rice was moved back into SuperSeg. He had been convicted of murder and put on death row. Rickie had helped influence some other SuperSeg inmates to become Christians and they were all praying for Tony to become a Christian and also to get off death row. The death row part of their prayers was answered and Tony was housed in the cell next to Rickie's, but he was certainly not a Christian. Rickie was 'jumping with joy' and praising God. He told Tony, "We have been praying for you and God answered our prayers and got you off death row."

"God did not get me off death row," Tony yelled, "The appeals court did!"

Rickie said, "You remember that Bible you threw out? God used that Bible and saved me."

Tony got mad, but Rickie let it go and didn't say any more about God. The air was thick between them. Rickie thought about writing to Price and Buenatello to cancel the plans for transferring him, because he was determined to change Tony's mind about God. He prayed even more for Tony as did the other Christians in SuperSeg.

Tony had become obsessed with working out. He would spend his whole recreation time doing pullups and pushups besides exercising in his cell. But he got ill and couldn't keep up the physical exertion. His breathing became difficult and he started coughing up phlegm. As Rickie was being escorted to recreation one day, he called out to Tony as they passed his cell but there was no answer, so he asked an officer to check.

The officer woke Tony up and saw that he was alive. He told him Rickie was concerned.

When Rickie returned from recreation, Tony jumped up, "Christianity has messed up your head," he yelled. "What you mean sending laws to my cell?"

Rickie responded with a quiet, "I'm sorry, Tony."

Two days later, Tony beat on the wall between their cells. He could barely talk. In a raspy voice he asked Rickie to get help. Officers came and took him to the infirmary. Rickie prayed more than he slept that night. In his spirit he seemed to be hearing that Tony had AIDS. But that didn't make sense to him since Tony was quite muscular and looked extremely healthy. The next day, Rickie told Rudy, another new Christian, what he was hearing and Rudy dismissed it, "That's the devil talking."

Two days later, the lieutenant came into SuperSeg and Rickie asked when Tony was coming back. "He may not come back. He's is in John Sealey Hospital in Galveston, in a coma, dying of AIDS."

Rickie was devastated. "Why," he asked God, "would you let Tony off death row, send him back to SuperSeg where he rejected you, and get sent to hell? I'm crushed and God, I'm mad at you."

Rickie, Rudy, and a couple of others prayed through a prayer list that included Tony at the same time twice each day. Three weeks later, Tony was returned to the cell next to Rickie. "I got good news and bad news, Rickie—which do you want first?"

"I always prefer good news first."

"The good is—Jesus saved me. I was in a coma, they said, and it was like someone run a video of everyone sharing Jesus with me, starting with my grandma when I was a little kid. Mark, a guy on death row with me, talked about Him. The last one on the video was you. Then a voice said, 'Now what are you going to do? Choose this day!' and I chose Jesus. The bad news is I got AIDS."

"Oh Lord," Rickie said with tears flowing, "I'm sorry for doubting Your love. Forgive me, Lord, and thank you for answering our prayers." The relief and happiness was soon tempered with Tony's bad news—AIDS. The medicine he was provided helped and they spent much of each day at the door of their cells talking about the Bible.

Concern for Tony's health and helping him mature as a Christian got Rickie thinking about his impending move. He decided it would be better for him to stay in SuperSeg with Tony. He was preparing to write to Warden Price and Sammy Buenatello to say he didn't want to be shipped to Darrington. He told that to Tony who reacted with shock. Rickie responded that he didn't want them to be separated.

"Oh, ye of little faith," Tony blurted out, quoting Jesus rebuking His disciples in Mathew, chapter 16. "If God wants us to stay together, He's big enough to move me to Darrington with you."

"I guess you're right," Rickie said haltingly. But, a week or so later, Tony got worse and was taken back to John Sealy Hospital. His property was left in cell # 3. Next day, Rickie was taken out for recreation. An officer commented that he heard he was getting out of SuperSeg.

"Yes, I was going to turn it down to stay here with Tony. But then we agreed that if God wants us to stay together, Tony will get moved to Darrington, too."

The officer laughed and said, "Fat chance." Then he took Rickie to shower. Right after putting him back in cell # 2, the phone on the table rang. They told the officer Tony would not be coming back and to pack up the property in # 3 and fill out tags with 'Destination Darrington Unit.'

The officer came to Rickie's cell and told him, with tears streaming down his face, "Please pray for me and my wife. I was raised a Christian but we have backslidden badly." Rickie touched his fingers through the bars and prayed. He, too, had tears streaming down his face.

So much for the meanest man in Texas prison!

CHAPTER EIGHTEEN

"Hey, Smith, get up and get ready! It's movin' day!" yelled an officer standing in front of the cell. It's 4:30 AM in midsummer 1991.

Rickie said, "I'm ready, let's go." He grabbed his few belongings, mostly bibles.

Then began the long, slow routine of moving an inmate in the Super Segregation unit. Finally a guard on each side begin walking slowly with the inmate—who is shuffling more than walking. They stop at each door to wait for it to open, then step through the door and stop for it to close, then repeat that for another door.

They proceed along a hallway, nodding to an occasional guard and watching a number of inmates they meet or who passes them. There's always activity in prisons, even in the middle of the night, and especially by five or six in the morning.

After going through the last doors, Rickie was ushered into a prison van, still guarded by two officers. A feeling of fear flashed through his mind as he noticed another inmate already in the van. It's Big Dan, Big Dan, a 6-foot, 8-inch, 375 pound 'ball of muscle.' Like Rickie, Big Dan came to prison with a short sentence and added hundreds of years for fighting officers. After he kicked two cell doors off their tracks, he was moved to SuperSeg escorted by the warden and assistant warden, and about twenty-five officers in full riot gear.

When Rickie saw him coming into the block, he shouted, "I got me some help now. You turkeys are in trouble!"

But Big Dan shouted back, "I'm done fighting laws!"

"You are a big old #$%&@! (a word meaning sissy)!" This was obviously before Rickie became a Christian and he set about to make Big Dan break out and come after him. He had a knife ready for the fight. There was much verbal taunting from cell to cell, with Rickie calling Dan everything he could think of trying to set him off. Once, Big Dan was taken to the shower and Rickie was able to fish his tennis shoes from outside the shower. He tied the size eighteen-and-a-half shoes to his cell door and set them on fire. Also, one day, Dan's visitation list was given to Rickie either by mistake or on purpose. So Rickie took off all the names of visitors he would accept, including family, and put new ones—David Duke and other KKK people he could think of. None of that or other things he tried would get Dan riled up to do something. Later, Rickie filed a lawsuit about Super Segregation and it caused everyone but him to be moved. The name of the cell block was officially changed to 'A-Side Segregation' and the lawsuit was ruled moot. In the move, Dan was taken to a different unit.

After the few seconds it took for Rickie's mind to review all that while getting into the van, he thought, *Here he sits and I don't have a handcuff key or even a knife to defend myself. He can smash me like a bug.* As he sat down, he said, "Dan, please forgive me for all that I did and tried to do to you. I am a Christian now, and that's all behind me."

"Thank God! Youse was a monster," was the reply. They both laughed. As they drove through the East Texas countryside, Rickie talked to Dan about Jesus until he was taken out at a prison unit at Huntsville.

The trip from Northeast Texas through Huntsville and Houston to Rosesharon took over three hours. For Rickie it was a wonderful ride, in spite of security and handcuffs. He was thanking God over and over for getting him out of SuperSeg and for the opportunity to clear the air and witness to Big Dan and especially for the bonus of having already moved his friend, Tony, to the Darrington Unit. He felt refreshed and excited and enjoyed the sights and scenery along the way—some in the Houston area he recognized from that "other life" before prison.

The van pulled into a secure driveway and the process was reversed for unloading Rickie at his new home. He barely got inside the main building at the Darrington Unit when he was put into a cage of heavy wire. Rickie anxiously waited for some official acknowledgement of his becoming the newest inmate.

After about an hour watching people coming and going in the hall without paying any attention to him, Rickie called to an officer who ignored him. Tired of standing in one place, he tried to move around enough to sit on the floor. There wasn't room to bend his legs and squat. He could only stand. He wanted to move around and would like to go to the bathroom, but still no one would answer him. He prayed for strength and especially for patience. This went on for hours. People walked by like he wasn't there and would not respond to him.

Finally, he saw five men in riot gear, including helmets, coming down the hall. They stopped at the cage, opened the door, ordered Rickie to turn around, and cuffed his hands behind his back. They added leg shackles then surrounded him. Two grabbed each arm and almost carried him down the hall and into a segregation cell block, called B-Line. He was finally unshackled and released into the last cell, through several inches of water. Fortunately, there was a toilet on the wall he could use, then tried to assess his situation.

Water covered the floor of the whole cell block. Noise of yelling and cursing was almost deafening—louder than SuperSeg. There was no lightbulb but just enough light to see the walls and ceiling were black from smoke, except where covered by feces smeared on the wall. Rickie felt the opposite of the excitement he had the first half of the day, joyfully thanking and praising the Lord. His high hopes for beginning a new and better life were drowning in filthy, sewer-smelling water.

He cried out, "Lord what have you done to me? SuperSeg was way better than this." Just then, a light came on out in the cell block sending a small shaft of light through a crack in the door, hitting a place on the wall where someone had drawn a cross. He dropped to his knees in the water mess, saying, "Oh Lord, forgive me. I know that You know what You're doing. I'm sorry for expecting you to do things my way. Please help me, Lord, to look to you, wait on you, trust you." He was very tired and decided to call it a day, in spite of the loud commotion outside his cell.

While eating some breakfast, Rickie reviewed his circumstances. The water on the floor was pretty much gone, thankfully. He still was haunted by disappointment in going from bad to worse. He came with high hopes, even thinking that Warden Price might welcome him to Darrington. He got to the door and began greeting those around him, to get acquainted with his new neighbors. He quickly found out he already knew most of them. Eight of the twelve first floor cells of B-line were occupied by Aryan Brotherhood gang members. Most inmates on the second level were Texas Mafia—Hispanic gang—and the top row was mostly Mandingo Warriors—black gang members. The gang wars were alive and well in B-Line. The flood when he arrived was Mandingo Warriors' primary weapon. They would cover the toilet drains and run the water until it flooded, down on the second floor and then mostly to the first floor. Aryan Brotherhood's weapon was to burn mattresses, sheets, or anything else to smoke out everyone above them.

Apparently, Warden Price put the worst troublemakers into B-Line where whatever they do to each other didn't affect the rest of the prisoners. So Darrington was as calm and secure as any other prison unit, except for the isolated B-Line cell block. And Rickie Smith found himself in the middle of the most active gang war in all of Texas prisons.

Daily recreation was outside in fenced areas with inmates assigned to recreation groups by gangs, so Rickie was in an AB group. That first day he was taken to the rec yard and immediately greeted with, "Hey, Buffalo (an old nickname), we're glad you pulled a rabbit out of the hat so you could join us." They assumed his becoming a Christian was a scam to get out of SuperSeg. He had written letters telling AB members that he had become a Christian and could not be in the gang.

"It wasn't a rabbit—it's Jesus," he replied emphatically, "I really am a Christian."

A guy called Wolf came over, patted Rickie on the back, "You'll be OK. You just been in SuperSeg too long."

One named Butcher agreed with Wolf. Butcher was the youngest and the fairest with blond hair and very blue eyes. He had lightning bolts tattooed from his armpits to his waist. "Butcher, it's not the color of our skin or our eyes that will gain favor with God," Rickie said sincerely. "It's a new heart that only Jesus can give us."

Some wandered off to resume exercising or chatting in clumps, But Rickie visited with Butcher. He learned Butcher had a nice wife and a two-year-old girl. He only had a five-year sentence but was a real troublemaker, an AB member, and soon ended up on B-Line. "Please stop, Butcher, or you'll ruin your life and end up like me. Accept Jesus as your Savior and He'll help you change so you can get out and have a good life." (Apparently the advice was ignored: Butcher kept causing trouble and getting more and more years added to his prison time—like Rickie.)

Rickie realized that he was much safer in SuperSeg than here on B-Line. But he still felt compelled to talk about Jesus. Since the AB guys wouldn't listen, he went to the fence and started visiting with some Mandingo Warriors in the next yard.

A little later, Wolf came up, "It's bad enough that you're a Christian, but here you are trying to save these black-gang guys that we're trying to kill."

Rickie said, "Since you don't want to hear about Jesus, I have to tell others. I just can't help it. I think I'd burst if I don't tell someone." So it went for days. Rickie was feeling wary of his former gang buddies and everyone else he was around. More than once, some inmates would climb the fence into the next rec yard to assault rival gangs. He generally felt alone. But he also was pleased to see that he handled all this in stride. He didn't get angry, he felt no hatred toward even those who criticized him. And, thankfully, he hadn't had any serious challenges from other convicts.

After a week or so, Warden Price had Rickie brought to the office and briefly acknowledged that he was there at Darrington. Several weeks later, the warden called him out again. This time was a serious meeting. There was a "hit letter" ordering Rickie to be killed, apparently by someone in Aryan Brotherhood.

"I'll move you out of B-Line and take away the handcuffs and extra security," Price said. Rickie smiled and thanked him. Price continued, "Now, you can go down there and beat someone up or kill an officer or another inmate. But one thing you won't be able to do is say you were never given a chance. God has given you a new start and I have given you a new start. Now it's up to you to take advantage of it."

"I am grateful to God and to you, Warden," Rickie said. "And I promise you that I will not fight or attack anyone. I give my word I will not let you down."

Such a contrast in E-Line cell block after moving from B-Line. A larger, cleaner cell; no constant yelling and cussing; no flood or smoke attacks; more freedom to move around, go to the dayroom; officers who generally seemed to like their jobs. E-Line was still a high security, management cell block, but much better than B-Line and SuperSeg. Freedom to move around was limited to the cell block and certain hours. The boost in his spirits was attributable even more to his attitude. In contrast to before, he liked people. He enjoyed talking with them, listening to them, and most of all sharing God's love and scriptures with them, whether inmate or officer—no longer thought of as "goons." He uses cell time reading the Bible and studying commentaries. Reading was still a challenge, but one he enjoyed and was improving at. Mike Barber, football star turned evangelist, provided study helps as did others.

Rickie enjoyed renewed visits with his mother. Selestia was ecstatic over her 'sweet little boy' turning his life around. A highlight each week for Rickie was a church service in the E-line dayroom. Various inmates would read scripture, give testimonies, and they did lots of praying and worshiping but on their own without a chaplain. But this was still prison and for most guards and inmates, Rickie Smith was still known as an

Aryan Brotherhood Gang member and, in court records, "the most violent man in Texas prison." He was, or had been, on at least five hit lists, including from the gang he bailed out of. And now, he had promised the warden that he would not fight anyone.

Rickie had asked about Tony Rice and learned that a few days before Rickie arrived at Darrington, Tony was found unconscious in his cell and had been taken to the hospital. They said a fungus was growing in his brain. Meningitis, apparently part of his AIDS, had caused it. He learned that most people in that condition never wake up out of the coma. Tony was in a coma several months and then did wake up. He was in the hospital another two months, recovering. Rickie regularly wrote to the chaplain and to Warden Price, asking about his friend. He kept Tony on the prayer list in the Sunday services and among his Christian friends.

He also questioned God, "What's the point? Why did you move Tony, then me, to Darrington then let him go into a coma? We had plans to bring Christ to the Texas Mafia and Aryan Brotherhood gang people, but he's stuck in the hospital—apparently dying." Rickie had been effective in reaching some gang and former gang members, but was sure that it would have even more impact if Tony was ministering with him.

Finally, Tony was moved back to Darrington, in E-pod, next to Rickie. They had a day or so to fellowship and pray together. And Rickie gave back the Bible Tony had discarded and ended up helping Rickie find salvation. But then Tony got worse—his brain was failing—and soon died.

Rickie and Warden Price had many visits. One time, Rickie accused the warden of not doing things in a Christlike manner. Price reminded him that his job was to run a prison—a tough, maximum-security prison. Also, he had to be careful of gang members playing like they had become Christians to get on E-wing to attack Rickie and other Christians. Whenever he had sufficient evidence of sincerity, he would move an inmate to E-line where he knew others would help him in the faith. He told Rickie he was very supportive of his ministry to ex-gang members. Christians would get moved to a row three cell. Rickie was in cell one and a strong Christian out of the Mexican Mafia was in number two. They partnered in discipling new believers. But it wasn't always peace and quiet. There were also frequent conflicts between inmates from various gangs who were housed in E-wing together and who were not part of the Christian group. There were flare-ups among themselves and anti-Christian attacks. Rickie was always careful to avoid getting into fights, as he had promised the warden. He stated his personal position but refused to let his dislike of others' opinions grow into a confrontation.

Rickie also spent a lot of time in studying and learning how to help others, as well as grow in his own relationship with the Lord. A well-known Christian artist, Barbara Fairchild, had become involved in prison ministry. Warden Price gave permission for the chaplain to bring her to E-wing to sing and speak with the inmates. She also sent a case of study Bibles and books for them to use. Rickie read a poem he had written and she wanted to buy it. He just gave it to her and she put it to music and recorded it.

Another woman in the ministry was involved. Wanda, the one who had joined Rickie and his dad praying in the SuperSeg visiting room, would come. Her church encouraged her to take as much time as possible going into prisons—gave her a van to help her. She continued to bring Red and Selestia to visit Rickie in Darrington. She also brought families of other converted gang members for visits. Many families of gang members would cut ties to their sons, but she would go to their house and tell them that their family member had become a new "creature" and convince them to go with her to see them and help in reconciliation. Rickie was impressed that she had spiritual insights to recognize when he was struggling with something and helped him with it.

In chapter 12, Royce Smithey was mentioned as part of the governor's prosecution team in Rickie's trials. He was the one Rickie looked at as a trial ended and said, "I'll just kill you." He then smuggled a 'shank' into the courtroom to use on Smithey in the next trial, but that was the trial when the judge ruled that he had to stay in chains with the 'box' over his hands which kept him from using the knife.

One day, Smithey was at Darrington Unit in regard to an inmate with an upcoming trial. He spoke to Warden Price who asked him if he remembered Rickie Smith. Even though it's five years later and he dealt with hundreds of inmates every year, he said, "Oh yes, I certainly remember him, one of the most dangerous in the whole system."

"Well, I think you'll be surprised if you talk with him. Would you like to talk with him?"

"Sure, I'll talk to him."

The warden called for Rickie to be brought up. He was sitting in his cell when an officer called out, "Smith, you have a visitor. Come on." And he opened the cell door.

"A visitor? Who? It's not the weekend."

"I don't know. They just called you out for an attorney visit."

"I don't have one. I don't want to go." Rickie knew this was something unusual.

"Too bad, you're going anyhow." He was taken to a cage for legal visits and sat for 10 minutes wondering what was happening to him now. He was very anxious and prayed, "Lord, help me. Please don't let me mess up if this is bad news."

Finally, Smithey came in with the assistant warden.

Oh no, not him! This guy is trouble, Rickie thought, then asked, "What do you want?"

"I heard you became a Christian—is this true?" Smithey asked.

Rickie nervously drawled out a long, "Yesss...."

"How did that happen?"

So Rickie told a short version of his conversion and could see a tear come out of Smithey's eye so asked, "Are you a Christian? How did that happen?"

"Yeah, Rickie, I am." And he explained how he had become an alcoholic, his marriage fell apart, and, "I called on Jesus to help me." The tension disappeared.

"Praise God!"

Smithey noticed that Rickie looked directly into his eyes as he talked, not through him as before in courtrooms. He was moved by the remorse he felt from Rickie. He thought, *I never saw remorse in the three cases we tried him for—stabbing two correctional officers and an inmate. How refreshing to see the joy he has.* He just sat back, listened, and enjoyed Rickie's joy and excitement. They talked an hour-and-a-half. Rickie used the opportunity to ask forgiveness for the way he had hated Smithey just for doing his job.

After the visit, Smithey went back to Warden Price to express his excitement at the difference in Rickie Smith. "I feel like it's sincere, his tree has fruit on it," Price said.

"Well, that's the only way we can really gauge a person—to look at their fruit."

Then Smithey thought that to hear that from such a veteran correctional person really validated the sincerity that he had felt from Rickie himself.

Price referred to the past when Rickie was in the racist Aryan Brotherhood, then said, "Now when he meets blacks in the prison, he'll preach to them. He'll say, 'One time if I met you, I'd try to stab you or hurt you or kill you, but now I want you to forgive me. I forgive you and I hope you forgive me. If you will let Him, Jesus Christ will save your soul. I'll help you get to know Him if you'll let me." Then Price added, "The prison environment is so tough, with evil all around you, it's hard to walk in faith—harder than for you and me, so-called 'free people.' It's such a credit to his testimony for him to be in the position he's in and still continue to grow in Christ."

In E Pod, officially E-Line, Rickie was friends with all the inmates, except the few who would not be friends. He talked about Jesus to all who would listen, regardless of any gang affiliation. Some leaders of the Texas Mafia gang (TM) got mad at Rickie and ordered a "hit" on him. That was because he and other Christians had led three TM members to accept Christ and join with the Christians. Warden Price would move inmates around to help the new Christians to have Bible study and mentoring and to get them away from the anti-Christian inmates. The three new believers from TM were moved to the third level of the cell block with other Christians. That apparently was a sign of losing a battle, so instructions were sent out to kill Rickie. They also issued instructions for someone to kill Selestia, Rickie's mother, whenever she came to visit and some member would be in a position to attack her. They even informed Rickie of those plans through the fence at recreation. Not long after that, Rickie was escorted to recreation when another officer left a gate open while escorting TM inmates to recreation at the same time. That left Rickie vulnerable to attack by a bunch of TM for some time. But nothing happened, which shocked Rickie. He attributed their missed opportunity to interference by the Holy Spirit.

When they had gotten so mad at Rickie, the Texas Mafia leader was called "Clutch." He had been approved for parole and was waiting to get out of prison. One day at recreation, Rickie talked to Clutch through the fence. He said, "You've made parole, but you need Jesus."

"What for?" he blurted. "I got a bad-a__ ole lady, a stripper. She bought land and put a new trailer house on it." She also got him a Harley Davidson and new pickup. "I got a job laying bricks at $32 an hour. I have a master's degree in business and I'm going to start my own business. What do I need Jesus for?"

Rickie felt the Holy Spirit urge him, "You are going to come back with a murder case because of your temper."

Clutch was furious, "That's why I don't like talking to you Christians. You're always trying to scare us with negative junk like He never spoke to Rickie again. That is, until after he had been home for sixty-three days and killed another TM gang member while with two other members who told on him. Then Clutch wrote to Rickie from county jail and said, "OK! How do I meet this Jesus friend of yours?"

Rickie wrote a letter similar to the one he had received from Bob Norris three years before. The charge against Clutch carried the death penalty as a 'gang-related' murder. But the two witnesses had drug charges and both lied on the stand in those cases and couldn't be used to try Clutch. Instead he was offered five years for manslaughter and took it. He was out in a few years and went to live with his mother.

Apparently, Clutch also followed up on Rickie's letter to him. His mother wrote Rickie and thanked him for "giving my son back." She was a Christian and corresponded with Rickie for years. Clutch became a committed believer and, incidentally, got the Texas Mafia hit on Rickie and his mother canceled. In the process, he shared the gospel with the other TM members.

CHAPTER NINETEEN

One day, Warden Price had Rickie brought to his office from E-Line cell Block. "You have been here a couple of years, Rickie, and you have done good. I'm convinced you're a different person. But most others don't see you differently. I tried to get you moved from ad-seg into general population. It was turned down because Darrington has so many gang-related convicts."

Rickie said, "I thank you very much for everything you've done. But it's OK, I'm fine on E-Line."

Price continued, "I'm moving in a few weeks to a new unit and I'll get you moved because it has a different makeup of inmates."

Rickie left the warden's office thinking, *Well, I guess we'll see how that works out.* Then he prayed, silently, "OK, Jesus, if you want to move me, that's fine. If not, I'll keep serving you here at Darrington. Oh, yes, Lord, thank you for Warden Price, and please take care of him in whatever's coming up."

In November 1993, Price moved to open the new Terrell Unit. It was designed specifically for maximum security, including death row. It was natural to choose a warden with a proven record for handling the toughest guys—Warden Keith Price. A month after opening the Terrell Unit, Price got Rickie transferred as promised. He was housed in an Administrative Segregation cell block, similar to E-line at Darrington, but the new design and more windows made it more comfortable. And in a few months he was upgraded to General Population and much more freedom—going to the cafeteria for meals, movement in the hallways, and a job. He was assigned to the laundry room, but it wasn't long until he was running errands for the office staff, including Warden Price.

Of course Rickie's reputation followed him. Some officers were wary of him and some watched closely to see if he might violate some rule—and lose his new freedom. A visiting warden came into Price's office one day while Rickie was hanging pictures on the wall. He immediately challenged Rickie for not being in lockup. Price quietly told Rickie to leave and then had "conversation" with the visitor—who had some personal history with the old Rickie but had no authority at the Terrell Unit.

Next, there was an opening for an inmate clerk in the chaplain's office and Rickie got it. He worked hard and concentrated to do a good job, overcoming the issues of dyslexia and a very poor seventh grade education. He loved it. He was in the middle of the Christian activity of the prison, set up the all-purpose room for chapel services learning from the chaplains and volunteer chaplains. He learned to handle the paperwork for various aspects of chaplain duties. He was constantly thankful to the Lord for this new life—the best in his forty years.

He came in before anyone else each morning and had his own prayer time—usually on the floor of the gym. It was an 'all-purpose' room including becoming the chapel for services. On Sunday and some other days, he and another inmate would set up the chairs and a platform for the services scheduled. He would make coffee and get messages and other things together for the chaplain's arrival. Chapel services were always a treat to Rickie. He would lead singing sometimes. Usually an inmate or two would sing a solo and some would give their testimony and then he loved the sermons by the regular chaplain or a volunteer.

(During this period, TDCJ increased the number of chaplains. Most units would have a Catholic and a Protestant chaplain. After longtime director of Chaplains, Emmett Soloman, retired, religious activity became less of a priority. Eventually, some units would have a single chaplain who served all different faiths.)

A new Protestant Chaplain, Dan Chapman, came had pastored Baptist churches for eighteen years before coming to TDCJ. He was very thankful for Rickie and the other inmate helper, Oscar Navarro.

"They answered a lot of questions I had on protocol and procedures. They helped me a great deal in getting adjusted. From there, our relationship began to grow in trust and also respect."

One thing he learned was about "jailhouse religion" as some inmates come and act like they belong for whatever advantage they might expect to get. "That's probably just like in the outside world—some come to church for their own reasons. Others are quite sincere in their faith. Jailhouse religion never lasts, but true faith will last."

Eventually, Warden Price enabled Rickie to add a new and exciting dimension to his ministry activities. He was allowed freedom to go almost anywhere in the Terrell Unit, including the segregation cell blocks where inmates are locked up all the time, like Rickie had been for many years. He visited them through the bars and tried to help them understand that life can be better if they give up the anger and violence as he had. For any who would listen, he talked about Jesus as the key to making that change. He was instrumental in a number of violent gang members asking Jesus into their life and becoming Christians.

A four-wheel cart was built for him so he could carry bibles and Christian literature into the cell blocks to distribute to all who would take them. That added even more joy and excitement to his new life. But there were also reminders of his previous life. He was cussed out and spit on, but he would respond kindly and move to the next cell. Outside the segregation cell blocks, former enemies would sometimes challenge him, confront him, even attack him. Occasionally, officers would make ugly remarks or try to accuse him of violating rules. Often, they were trying to provoke him to attack. Even some newer inmates would seek out the "great Rickie Smith" to try to whip him and thereby gain in their own tough reputation. A few times Rickie would stand his ground like he would take them on but they always backed down. He let them know up front that he was not the same guy and that he did not want any trouble.

Those he had history with he asked forgiveness for attacking or even trying to kill them. When appropriate, he would just stand meekly and tell the challengers to do what they have to do because he would not resist. He was determined to keep his promise to Warden Price to not attack or fight anyone. And in every instance the confrontation ended without a physical fight. Rickie always asked the Lord to guide him and protect him in those times and he was always thankful in the outcomes.

Not that it was easy. For years his first reaction had been to prove himself as a 'stand-up-guy' and punish whoever showed him disrespect. But he became more sensitive to those feelings and overcame them with his desire to be faithful to God and his promise to Warden Price.

He loved trying to get through to inmates with the Gospel message, sometimes spending all day in the lockdown cell blocks. Often, he was accompanied by Baptist Evangelist, Al Gibbons, "Chaplain Al," who has a headquarters in East Texas, and came regularly as a volunteer chaplain.

Wanda would bring eighty-four-year-old Selestia to visit. Rickie thought many times how lucky he was to still have his mother. He said, "Everyone else gave up on me, except my mom and Jesus." Red would also come to visit, enjoying the fellowship they never had as a family. And Becky showed up, too. It seems that she and Jeff couldn't get along after all. In fact she left him after he beat her up and was awaiting trial on some federal charges. She apologized to Rickie for the way she had treated him and became interested when they talked about the Lord.

One of the 'hits' (kill orders) on Rickie pretty much resolved itself. He had accused a Texas Syndicate member of being the snitch that got Becky caught smuggling drugs and given a prison term. The syndicate put the hit on Rickie. However, later there was unrelated trouble with the officers and the syndicate discovered that the inmate really was a snitch. So the hit was taken off Rickie and put on the snitch.

The Aryan Brotherhood still had Rickie on a hit list, because he quit the gang after becoming a Christian. He had already cleared that with Jeff Lykens and some other gang members. But one day he went out in the yard at Terrell surrounded by twenty-three AB gang members. Rickie told them, "I am a Christian now and cannot be in the gang. I will never snitch on you or even discuss your business, but if ya'll want to kill me and send me to Jesus today—I'm ready! If not, I'll stay out of your business. I'm only about God's business now."

They accepted that and respected him for being frank with them. And of course he invited all of them to come to church. There were a few minor clashes with some AB, but generally they left him alone.

Not long after that, the founder of the Mandingo Warriors (black gang), Kenneth, had been moved from SuperSeg to Terrell and eventually into general population. He worked in the kitchen. He was wiping tables one day when Rickie came up behind him and tapped his shoulder. He didn't recognize Rickie at first but then said, "You could have killed me."

"I'm a Christian now. I don't want to kill anyone. All that stuff is behind us. I wish you well and, by the way, come to church Sunday and hear my testimony." Kenneth didn't come to church, but that last gang hit order went away.

The rest of any challenges to Rickie were individual disagreements and he handled them as he had been—walking away or standing his ground, always explaining he was only involved in God's business. He was always able to keep his promise to Warden Price to not attack or fight. But he was very concerned for weaker brothers who were mistreated. For example, a young Christian inmate came to church after being gang-raped. Rickie got an official pass and put a bunch of Christians' names on it. They went to the young guy's wing and put him in the middle of the dayroom, surrounded by the others. They laid hands on him and prayed for his protection and promised they were all together with their brothers as the Lord led them. That demonstration of concern and solidarity ended the attacks on that inmate.

Here's a creative example of deflecting fights while not being a sissy: a new 'tough guy' inmate got a hold on Rickie and said, "Give me your commissary card or I'll break your neck."

Rickie said OK and got loose enough to pull out his card. Then he tore it in pieces rather than give it to the attacker. So there was nothing to fight over. Of course Rickie could not buy anything until he went through the process to have it replaced.

In 1995 Rickie's dad, T. R. Smith, passed away. It was a difficult time, but his consolation came from knowing his dad was now in heaven with the Lord he had accepted three years earlier at Coffield.

Fifteen wardens came to Terrell one day for a meeting. As they were passing the chaplain's office, Warden Jack Garner's cell phone rang and he stepped into the office. Rickie was at the desk and showed Garner into the chaplain's office to take the call. When Garner came out, Rickie felt a nudge from the Holy Spirit to talk to him. He apologized for all the trouble he had caused and asked forgiveness. He was the warden where Rickie stabbed a black inmate and held off officers for a while with a buck knife and a hoe. Also, it was Garner whom Rickie threw feces into his face and on his very nice suit. Rickie wasn't sure if his apology was fully accepted, but at least it was not rejected and he had done his part with another name on his forgiveness list. He was fully convinced the Lord had brought that opportunity to him.

Sometime later, Warden Price moved to the Coffield Unit. He could not take Rickie with him because of his history there, in SuperSeg. Price was replaced at Terrell by Warden James Shaw. Soon after the change, Rickie was lying on his belly in the all-purpose room for his early morning praying.

A voice said, "Get up, son." Rickie first thought it was Jesus. Then he saw it was Warden Shaw. "You really have changed," the Warden said.

"I really love Jesus, if that's what you mean" was Rickie's response. Before Shaw arrived, an assistant warden, Bruce Zeller, was in charge and he took away most of Rickie's special privileges. Shaw reinstated them all which made Zeller very angry. He could do nothing about it at that time, but several years later Zeller had his opportunity.

After a couple of years at Terrell Unit, Warden Shaw was promoted to regional director. But before he left, he arranged through the Classification Office for Rickie to transfer to the Retrieve Unit where he would have the same job as clerk in the chaplain's office. This put him out of the reach of Assistant Warden Zeller. Since the orders came from Huntsville (headquarters), officers and inmates alike would ask, "Who are you?" or "Who do you know?" This made Rickie a bit uneasy, but he trusted the Lord and served Him in this new home.

When he was first moving in, some asked if he knew he will be working with a black chaplain, apparently reacting to Rickie's history in the Aryan Brotherhood. A veteran major pressed him on it. "All I want to know is if he loves the Lord," Rickie said.

"Well, you'll have to ask him that," the major said.

The transition to Retrieve was not comfortable. But he and the chaplain got along good and the Lord used them in ministering. His circumstances at Retrieve never did get to the same level of comfort and joy he had at Terrell. But he enjoyed the Christians coming to chapel and focused on his work and brushed off all challenges and accusing remarks just as he had at Darrington and Terrell.

In 1999, Keith Price moved from the Coffield Unit to Amarillo, in the Texas Panhandle, as warden of the William Clements Unit. It was named for the Texas governor who had met with Federal Judge William Wayne Justice and helped break the stalemate which resulted in the chaotic transition that revolutionized the operation of the Texas prison system. Rickie requested a transfer to the Clements Unit and Price helped facilitate that move, putting them back together. This was Warden Price's final position in TDCJ before retirement and Rickie hoped it would be his final prison home.

The Clements Unit was a modern prison with one of the larger inmate capacities. Opened in 1990, a high security compound was added ten years later, shortly after Price became warden. Clements became known for using inmates in community service projects, including interstate highway landscaping, trails and camping sites in Palo Duro Canyon State Park, and many others. The prison received numerous awards and recognitions for these.

Rickie was comfortable and happy at Clements. He was involved in ministry in the chapel and in personal contacts. A craft shop was created and he began working in leather. He loved it and spent more and more time making boots, belts, and simpler leather goods. He was more relaxed and secure because he was again under his mentor, Warden Keith Price. But it was still prison, where life was not easy at best. There were all the security measures, rules and protocols, but also gang members and various inmates who held grudges, wanted to build a reputation, or just caused trouble. Also, there were officers, even in the far corner of the state, who remembered the old Rickie—by personal experience or by reputation. Of course, his prison record followed him everywhere.

So, every so often, Rickie had the opportunity to explain his Christian Faith and the changes to the "new Rickie." Sometimes it got dangerous, but he always remembered his promise to Warden Price as well as his faith that God would take care of him. He always came out without a fight and usually succeeded in telling someone new about Jesus.

CHAPTER TWENTY

K eith Price retired from the Texas Department of Criminal Justice in 2003.

He was aware that he would not get promoted higher than warden because of his work helping change the culture of the prison staff. Also, he was tiring of dealing with 'society's rejects' day after day, and it was discouraging that so few inmates achieve success after discharge from TDCJ and the lack of effective programs to change attitudes of convicts. He took an opportunity to try to influence prison dynamics as an associate professor, and soon professor of criminal justice at West Texas State University in Canyon, near Amarillo.

For Rickie, he not only lost his friend and mentor but was now under the control of his TDCJ "enemy." Bruce Zeller followed Price as warden of the Clements unit. He was skeptical of Price's treatment of Rickie Smith.

Rickie's life in prison followed much the same pattern already described through recent years—an occasional challenge from some other inmate, but also opportunities to talk about his Lord and Savior. Of course, like any Christian, there were times of discouragement or wanting to know why God hadn't answered his prayer the way he expected.

The first real challenge he had to deal with was Warden Zeller closing the craft shop. Rickie had been working hard there, with a backlog of orders for cowboy boots. He paid little attention when some officers would bring food into the shop, where they could cook things for lunch on a hot plate. But during an inspection, some hamburger meat was found, in violation of the rules. Since Rickie was the primary inmate using the craft shop, he was charged with having contraband. When he was questioned, he refused to tell on the officers who were responsible, which left him with the blame.

Zeller closed the craft shop and had it cleared out. That took away the opportunity for Rickie to make some spending money in his commissary account. Even worse, it removed the ability to do productive, creative, and enjoyable work, and contributed to a time of questioning God. But finding relevant scriptures and encouragement from Christian buddies helped him over that and back to his normal life and praising the Lord.

A more serious example of letting your feelings get in the way of your faith occurred sometime later, and it was life-changing. There was no one else to blame, this time, even if he wanted to. He was feeling continuing animosity from authorities in the Clements Unit. Then, some inmates with gang connections and history were transferred to Clements and stirred up others who were already there. They brought up some old threats aimed at Rickie. He told them, "That's all behind me years ago. I'm a Christian and all about Jesus, not any gang business."

"Yeah, I heard you were a goody two-shoes, but that doesn't cover the things you did to us. When the time's right, we'll take care of that," declared the leader.

The more their threats played in Rickie's head, and feeling exposed and alone since Warden Price retired, he got more concerned. Finally, he decided he needed some defense. He fashioned a "shiv" from a piece off the steel bunk so he would have something to try to keep the trouble-makers away. Before there was any confrontation with those inmates, a shakedown was ordered for the cell block where Rickie lived. He knew he would be removed from the cell and searched so he hid the knife in his typewriter. But in going through the cells, the knife was found and Rickie was written up for a major infraction. He was demoted to maxi-mum security and moved to the Allred Unit. It's back to the old routine of being locked in except for an hour of recreation and shower. Bruce Zeller, now promoted to regional director, told Rickie, "You will stay in maximum security until you die.

Rickie knew this was his own fault. He agonized over failing God in his lack of faith. There were so many times that God had protected him in similar situations, but this time Rickie overlooked that and relied on his own feelings. He asked for forgiveness, with many tears, and knew that God had forgiven him, but his failure still gnawed at him. He had plenty of time in his cell for Bible study, prayer, and meditation regarding faith and God's promises. His biggest regret was that after such an active Christian witness for many years, he had to start over to gain credibility as a faithful follower of Christ. He was determined to do it. On a human level it hurt deeply that a number of officers and administrators in TDCJ who were skeptical of his change of life as a Christian were able to say, "I knew it was not real."

He wrote to friends to tell them how humbled and ashamed he was. Their responses were to remind him no one can be perfect except Christ himself. They emphasized God's forgiveness, grace, and restoration. That encouragement helped him put the matter behind him and get into a routine of living in lockup. He took advantage of having more time for Bible study and prayer. He witnessed to others in the cell block and saw some make commitments to Christ. He got along with all the officers who worked a shift in the cell block. He could listen to Christian radio. So it went for several years. He kept a spotless record.

One day in the fall of 2017, Rickie was informed that he was moving back to the Clements Unit. He balked and said he had not asked for transfer and he didn't want to move. He was involved in a Bible study program he didn't want to leave. He was moved anyway. Then he learned he was in a TDCJ project that was designed to prepare maximum security inmates for future release from prison. Soon, he realized the material he studied was worthwhile. After six months, he had done well enough that he was informed that when he completed the course in eighteen months, he'd be eligible to be considered for parole.

The one time, previously, he had a date to be considered, Regional Director Zeller had it canceled. But this time Zeller was retired from TDCJ. When TDCJ reported to the Board of Pardons and Paroles that an inmate had served the time obligation and had met certain standards, his case could be set for a hearing. If the Board voted to recommend parole, it had to be accepted by the governor. The convict must have a verifiable plan, including a place to live and a job.

Rickie began praying and thinking about what he will do "in the free world." Not so much the place to live or a job—those had already been promised him by a pastor and Christian businessmen. But life outside was very different than it was forty years ago and an extreme change from living in confinement.

He loved working with vehicles, and had shown a real aptitude for it in his young years. He devoured all the magazines and catalogs he could get hold of. He even considered that it might be worth being in prison another year so he could take a High Performance Engine class which was offered at the Allred Unit.

His excitement grew. But through it all, he kept praying, "Lord, thank you for bringing this about." He knew only God could have made these changes in circumstances. "Whatever YOU want me to do on the outside comes first, ahead of anything else. Or even if you want me to stay in here longer, that's fine. I'll serve you here or out there. I trust you to open and close doors to make a path for me to walk and to serve you."

POSTLUDE

This book contains terrible activity and wonderful activity, and that's why I wrote it. The contrast is stark and I hope it comes through to you, the reader. Prison is a bad place to be, at best. Many inmates are able to stay in a peaceful routine and finish their sentences, but others, for whatever reason, become embroiled in conflict. I met Rickie in Super Seg in 1990 and have corresponded and visited him regularly, since. I also met his parents, wife Becky, Jack Wilcox, other chaplains and many others who knew him growing up and in prison. Becky and both parents are deceased.

This is not intended to be a textbook or an expose about prisons and the people who live or work there. This is a story of certain persons during a specific period of time. Most of the quotes are from interviews I did with those people or from trial transcripts. In a few instances, I made up a name or added some incidental activity just to make it a story. But nothing was done to add or detract from the reality of life as it is lived by some people in some prisons.

The title words "REAL PRISON" have two meanings, as you may have surmised. There are the physical prisons of The Texas Department of Criminal Justice, and Rickie Smith is still living there as I write. However, his worse imprisonment was the anger and hatred that motivated him in that awful existence and kept him from peace and happiness.

The other title words, "REAL FREEDOM", has one meaning.

Because Jesus changed Rickie's heart, he was freed from the bondage of rage, fear and pride. He has remained in TDCJ thirty years as a Christian, often in Maximum security lockup – but he is free in his heart and mind to enjoy interacting with people and especially fellowshipping with The Lord. He is nice to officers – even those who continue to treat him as the "old" Rickie. (Prison systems do not recognize 'religion' as an asset.) He has read and studied the Bible over and over and still gets excited over new lessons he finds there.

We would wish to analyze Rickie's life to determine the cause of the horrible years he suffered. Was it his dad's mistreatment? Could it be blamed on dyslexia and education problems? Might it be his parents fighting and divorce? Maybe too much doting and spoiling from his mother? Perhaps it was just the intersection of difficulties within the society at vulnerable times?

We'll never be able to assign proper blame. We could easily apply "or all the above." The bottom line is that Rickie made choices, mostly bad ones. God presented him with opportunities to know Him personally, over and over. However, like most of us, he held on to his own expectations and wishes of the nature of God, our Creator. We want God to be like us or like some problem-solving fictional superheroes, rather than give up our own lordship of our life. Rickie, like most of us, had to hit bottom and give up on using his own plans to pay attention to The Lord.

Rickie's story also helps us see that becoming a Christian does not immediately make us good and take away our problems. We, like Rickie, need to learn new ways of thinking and living as Christians. Too often, that is the deal breaker for 'seekers'. We must adjust to different motivations and purposes. We may also have to live with some consequences of previous mistakes.

There are people who wonder if God is real and my hope is that this book will help them see that He is real. The proof true Christians have of God's relationship with them is in their spiritual nature. I cannot take my spirit out and show you the proof. But, as Warden Price told Rickie, your actions will demonstrate the truth of your accepting Christ. That is why you have this book in your hands – because I want you to see the truth of God working in and through someone. As Rickie experienced, sincerely turning to the Lord brings His proof into you. That results in a new feel and attitude, followed by changes in life and actions.

Jesus, Himself, gave that explanation, in the temple at a Jewish Feast, recorded in John, chapter 7:16-17: **"My teaching isn't mine but is from the One who sent me. If anyone wants to do His will, he will understand whether the teaching is from God or if I am speaking on my own."** [HCSB] Our choosing to do God's will is the step of faith which starts the process. The beloved Apostle, John, in First John, chapter 3:24, puts it this Way: **"The one who keeps His commands remain in Him and He in him. And the wasy we know that He remains in us is from the Spirit He has given us."** [HCSB] The Apostle Paul describes the result in Romans, chapter 6, verse 16, **"Don't you know that if you offer yourselves to someone as obedient slaves, you are slaves of that one you obey – either of sin leading to death or of obedience leading to righteousness?"** [HCSB]

So as distasteful as the terrible parts of this true story are to us (and especially terrible for Rickie to talk about) the change in his life is demonstrated. And he much prefers his life as led by the Lord to the life he had made for himself. A difference we, and those who associate with him in prison, can recognize and appreciate. I can say that about my own life experience too.

Warden Keith Price is another graphic example of following God's direction in life and actions. There are others in this story who show that, too, in less detail.

We conclude with Rickie's testimony in his own words.

RICKIE TESTIMONY

November 28, 2019! Its Thanksgiving Day and I am so thankful today that even though I was dead in my transgressing sins, God extended His Grace and Mercy to this outlaw. In a special built cell, on February 2, 1990, I fell on my face in a dirty prison cell – I'd come to my end, out of gas. Sin and rebellion had destroyed my family and friends. My wife was in a prison cell, my precious adopted mom taken off my visitation list, from my selfish desires, and rebellion. Fighting with all authority and seeds sown had produced its crop of misery, suffering and hopelessness. Not only my pain and suffering, sin never comes single, never private, forget "I'm hurting nobody but myself".

My wife got 10 years for her part in smuggling drugs into Coffield Unit, as you read. I was a broken man, felt so low. I was a snake. There's a Led Zepplin song that says 'It's nobody's fault but mine". King David says "against You and You only have I sinned."

There was a stop sign in my life named Bob Norris who was faithful to our Lord and Savior, Jesus Christ. He wrote, under orders of the Holy Spirit, of God's Love, Mercy and REST! I was sick and tired, wore out, needed REST. Bob's first letter a couple of years before included a verse, 'come onto me all you that labor and are heavy laden and I will give you REST'. My Lord, Jesus, gives rest only when we get tired and hungry and thirsty. We can come to Him and get our fill and have sweet rest after we get a drink to quench our thirst, water AND NEW LIFE – EAT

OUR FILL OF HEAVENLY BREAD OF LIFE, sweet rest. You got to be hungry, thirsty and tired. But what about this 'sinner' stuff? Dead in my sins and transgressions. The Word says to cast from you your transgressions and get a new heart and spirit. Dictionary says transgressor is … lawbreaker, outlaw. Jesus volunteered to shed God's blood to purchase the church – His true church (not denominations). Well, it was my fists that beat Him, I was the spit and curses of the crowd crucifying Him. My sin and yours were in those words of the crowd of outlaws.

I once wrote down how I was there and what they did to Jesus and I included what I want to do for Him. A dear sister, Barbara Fairchild, saw it and wanted to buy it for a new gospel album. I said it is yours for free. She is one of many God brought into my life, including Warden Dr. Keith Price. I first met him in the outlaw days and then as a Christian. Another dear brother, Rosser McDonald who's writing this book, also did a documentary about my crazy outlaw life and the beginning of new life lived out still in prison.

You need to be careful about what you say in TDCJ. Recently, I mentioned to my roommate that this morning, "The Holy Spirit told me...." So, in the last thirty days I was assigned to a mental unit. Recently, my new next-door neighbor threw feces into my cell and on me. I started taking my little fan apart to use the motor to give him a tune-up. But I needed to repent as bad as he does, I got on my face on the dirty floor, asking to be a stop sign for people reading this book.

Please pray that I'll keep a soft heart, keep hearing from our Redeemer. I am glad to be counted crazy for Christ. We serve where we are at. There is no mistake I am just where my Lord wants me. I don't want to let the world, our fleshly desires or the pride of life ever keep me from hearing and obeying that voice. I pray that you will become a stop sign to others and to tell them where to find rest and REAL FREEDOM.

Rickie Smith

www.ingramcontent.com/pod-product-compliance
Ingram Content Group UK Ltd.
Pitfield, Milton Keynes, MK11 3LW, UK
UKHW031124120325
456135UK00006B/132